Foreign Office Great Britain

The official correspondence relative to the negotiation for peace between Great Britain and the French republic

Foreign Office Great Britain

The official correspondence relative to the negotiation for peace between Great Britain and the French republic

ISBN/EAN: 9783337150488

Printed in Europe, USA, Canada, Australia, Japan

Cover: Foto ©ninafisch / pixelio.de

More available books at **www.hansebooks.com**

THE
OFFICIAL CORRESPONDENCE

RELATIVE TO THE

NEGOTIATION FOR PEACE,

BETWEEN

GREAT BRITAIN AND THE FRENCH REPUBLICK.

AS LAID BEFORE BOTH

HOUSES OF PARLIAMENT,

BY

HIS MAJESTY's COMMAND.

LONDON:

PRINTED FOR J. WRIGHT,
14, OPPOSITE OLD BOND STREET, PICCADILLY.
1797.

LIST OF PAPERS

Presented by His MAJESTY's Command.

No. 1. OFFICIAL Note from Lord Grenville to the Minister for Foreign Affairs of the French Republick, dated Westminster, 1st June 1797.—And Translation.

No. 2. Official Note from the Minister for Foreign Affairs to Lord Grenville, dated Paris, 16 Prairial, 5th Year of the French Republic.—And Translation.

No. 3. Official Note from Lord Grenville to the Minister for Foreign Affairs, dated Westminster, 8th June 1797.—And Translation.

No. 4. Official Note from the Minister for Foreign Affairs to Lord Grenville, dated Paris, 23 Prairial, 5th Year.

No. 5. Passport.—And Translation.

No. 6. Official Note from Lord Grenville to the Minister for Foreign Affairs, dated Westminster, 17th June 1797.—And Translation.

No. 7. Official Note from the Minister for Foreign Affairs to Lord Grenville, dated Paris, 2 Messidor.—And Translation.

No. 8. Official Note from Lord Grenville to the Minister for Foreign Affairs, dated Westminster, 26th June 1797.—And Translation.

No. 9. Official Note from the Minister for Foreign Affairs to Lord Grenville, dated Paris, 11 Messidor, 5th Year.—And Translation.

No. 10. Extract of a Dispatch from Lord Malmesbury to Lord Grenville, dated Lisle, 6th July, Thursday, Eight P. M. 1797.

No. 11. Copy of the full Powers of the French Plenipotentiaries.—And Translation.

[vi]

No. 12. Extract of a Difpatch from Lord Malmefbury to Lord Grenville, dated Lifle, Tuefday, 11th July 1797.

No. 13. Copy of the Project delivered by Lord Malmefbury to the French Plenipotentiaries, 8th July 1797.—And Tranflation.

No. 14. Note from Lord Malmefbury to the French Plenipotentiaries, dated Lifle, the 8th July 1797.—And Tranflation.

No. 15. Note from the French Plenipotentiaries to Lord Malmefbury, dated Lifle, 21 Meffidor, 5th Year.—And Tranflation.

No. 16. Note from the French Plenipotentiaries to Lord Malmefbury, dated Lifle, 22 Meffidor, 5th Year.—And Tranflation.

No. 17. Extract of a Difpatch from Lord Grenville to Lord Malmefbury, dated Downing Street, 13th July 1797.

No. 18. Extract of a Difpatch from Lord Malmefbury to Lord Grenville, dated Lifle, 16th July 1797.

No. 19. Extract of a Difpatch from Lord Malmefbury to Lord Grenville, dated Lifle, 16th July 1797.

No. 20. Note from the French Plenipotentiaries to Lord Malmefbury, dated Lifle, 27 Meffidor, 5th Year.—And Tranflation.

No. 21. Note from Lord Malmefbury to the French Plenipotentiaries, dated Lifle, 15th July 1797.—And Tranflation.

No. 22. Note from the French Plenipotentiaries to Lord Malmefbury, dated Lifle, 27 Meffidor, 5th Year.—And Tranflation.

No. 23. Copy of a Difpatch from Lord Grenville to Lord Malmefbury, dated Downing Street, 20th July 1797.

No. 24. Copy of a Difpatch from Lord Grenville to Lord Malmefbury, dated Downing Street, 20th July, 1797.

No. 25. Extract of a Difpatch from Lord Malmefbury to Lord Grenville, dated Lifle, 25th July 1797.

No. 26. Note from Lord Malmefbury to the French Plenipotentiaries, dated Lifle, 24th July 1797.—And Tranflation.

No. 27.

[vii]

No. 27. Extract of a Difpatch from Lord Malmefbury to Lord Grenville, dated Lifle, Sunday, 6th Auguft 1797.

No. 28. Note from the French Plenipotentiaries to Lord Malmefbury, dated Lifle, 17 Thermidor, 5th Year.—And Tranflation.

No. 29. Extract of a Difpatch from Lord Malmefbury to Lord Grenville, dated Lifle, 14th Auguft 1797.

No. 30. Extract of a Difpatch from Lord Grenville to Lord Malmefbury, dated Downing Street, 19th Auguft 1797.

No. 31. Extract from the Meffage of the French Directory to the Council of Five Hundred of the 9th Auguft 1797—And Tranflation.

No. 32. Copy of a Difpatch from Lord Malmefbury to Lord Grenville, dated Lifle, 22d Auguft 1797.

No. 33. Extract of a Difpatch from Lord Malmefbury to Lord Grenville, dated Lifle, 22d Auguft 1797.

No. 34. Extract of a Difpatch from Lord Malmefbury to Lord Grenville, dated Lifle, 29th Auguft 1797.

No. 35. Extract of a Difpatch from Lord Malmefbury to Lord Grenville, dated Lifle, 5th September 1797.

No. 36. Extract of a Difpatch from Lord Malmefbury to Lord Grenville, dated Lifle, 9th September 1797.

No. 37. Extract of a Difpatch from Lord Grenville to Lord Malmefbury, dated Downing-Street, September 11th 1797.

No. 38. Copy of a Difpatch from Lord Malmefbury to Lord Grenville, dated Lifle, 11th September 1797.

No. 39. Note from the French Plenipotentiaries to Lord Malmefbury, dated Lifle, 25 Fructidor, 5th Year.—And Tranflation.

No. 40. Note from Lord Malmefbury to the French Plenipotentiaries, dated Lifle, 12th September 1797.—And Tranflation.

No. 41. Extract of a Difpatch from Lord Malmefbury to Lord Grenville, dated Lifle, 17th September 1797.

No. 42. Copy of a Difpatch from Lord Malmefbury to Lord Grenville, dated Lifle, 17th September 1797.

No. 43. Note from the French Plenipotentiaries to Lord Malmefbury, dated Lifle, the 29 Fructidor, 5th Year.—And Tranflation.

No. 44. Note from Lord Malmesbury to the French Plenipotentiaries, dated Lisle, 16th September, 1797.—And Translation.

No. 45. Note from the French Plenipotentiaries to Lord Malmesbury, dated Lisle, 30 Fructidor, 5th Year.—And Translation.

No. 46. Note from Lord Malmesbury to the French Plenipotentiaries, dated Lisle, 16th September 1797.—And Translation.

No. 47. Note from the French Plenipotentiaries to Lord Malmesbury, dated Lisle, 30 Fructidor, 5th Year.—And Translation.

No. 48. Note from Lord Malmesbury to the French Plenipotentiaries, dated Lisle, Sunday, 17th September 1797.—And Translation.

No. 49. Note from the French Plenipotentiaries to Lord Malmesbury, dated Lisle, 1st Complementary Day, 5th Year.—And Translation.

No. 50. Dispatch from Lord Grenville to Lord Malmesbury, dated Downing Street, 22d September 1797.

No. 51. Note from Lord Malmesbury to the French Plenipotentiaries, dated London, 22d September 1797.—And Translations.

No. 52. Note from the French Plenipotentiaries to Lord Malmesbury, dated Lisle, 4th Vendemiaire, 5th Year.—And Translation.

No. 53. Note from the French Plenipotentiaries to Lord Malmesbury, dated Lisle, 10th Vendemiaire, 6th Year.—And Translation.

No. 54. Note from Lord Malmesbury to the French Plenipotentiaries, dated London, 5th October 1797.—And Translation.

CORRESPONDENCE, &c.

Papers presented by His Majesty's Command.

(No. 1.) Official Note.—Lord Grenville to the Minister for Foreign Affairs of the French Republick.

LA Signature des Préliminaires d'une Paix, dont la Conclusion définitive doit terminer la Guerre du Continent, paroît offrir aux Deux Gouvernemens de la Grande Bretagne et de la France une Occasion naturelle et des nouvelles Facilités pour le Rénouvellement des Négotiations pacifiques entre eux:—Une Partie des Obstacles qui auroient pu retarder cet Ouvrage salutaire n'existant plus; et les Intérêts dont on aura à traiter depuis cet Evenement n'etant ni aussi étendus ni aussi compliqués qu'ils l'etoient auparavant.

La Cour de Londres desirant toujours employer tous les Moyens les plus propres à contribuer à cet Objet, si interessant pour le Bonheur des Deux Nations, n'a pas voulu omettre de renouveller au Gouvernement François l'Assurance de ses Dispositions constantes à cet egard. Et le Soussigné est autorizé de proposer au Ministre des Relations Exterieures d'entrer sans Délai, et sous telle Forme qui sera jugée la plus convenable, dans la Discussion des Vues et des Pretensions respectives, pour regler les Preliminaires d'une Paix, que l'on arrangeroit definitivement au Congrés futur.

Dés que l'on seroit d'accord sur la Forme de cette Négotiation, le Gouvernement Britannique seroit prêt à y concourir en prenant de sa Part toutes les

Mesures les plus propres pour accélérer le Rétablissement de la Tranquillité publique.

(Signé) GRENVILLE.

à Westminster, ce 1 Juin, 1797.

(No. 1.) Translation.

THE Signature of the Preliminaries of a Peace, the definitive Conclusion of which is to put an End to the Continental War, <u>appears to afford</u> to the Two Governments of Great Britain and France <u>a natural Opportunity and new Facilities for the Renewal of pacifick Negociations between them</u>: A Part of the Obstacles, which might have retarded this salutary Work, no longer existing; and the Interests to be treated of being, after this Event, neither so extensive nor so complicated as they were before.

The Court of London, always desirous of employing such Means as are best calculated to contribute to this Object, so interesting to the Happiness of the Two Nations, is unwilling to omit renewing to the French Government the Assurance of the Continuance of its Dispositions on this Subject. And the Undersigned is authorized to propose to the Minister for Foreign Affairs <u>to enter without Delay</u>, and in such Manner as shall be judged the most expedient, <u>upon the Discussion</u> of the Views and Pretensions of each Party for the Regulation of the Preliminaries of a Peace, which may be definitively arranged at the future Congress.

As soon as the Form of this Negotiation shall have been agreed upon, the British Government will be ready to concur in it, by taking on its Part such Measures as are the most proper for accelerating the Re-establishment of the public Tranquillity.

(Signed) GRENVILLE.

Westminster, June 1, 1797.

(No. 2.)   Official Note.—The Minister for Foreign Affairs to Lord Grenville.

Le Ministre des Relations Exterieures de la Republique Française soussigné s'est empressé de mettre sous les yeux du Directoire Exécutif la Note qui lui à été transmise le 1 Juin 1797 (v. st.) par le Lord Grenville, au Nom de Sa Majesté Britannique. Il est chargé d'y repondre.

Le Directoire Exécutif voit avec Satisfaction le Desir qu' annonce le Cabinet de Saint James de faire cesser enfin les Malheurs de la Guerre. Il accueillera avec Empressement les Ouvertures et les Propositions qui lui seront faites par la Cour d'Angleterre.

Le Directoire Exécutif desire, cependant, que les Negociations s'entament de suite pour un Traité Definitif. Cette Marche Lui paroit préférable à un Congrés, dont le Résultat ne peut qui être fort eloigné, et ne répond point au Desir ardent qu'il a de rétablir, le plus promptement possible, la Paix entre les Deux Puissances.

         (Signé)   CH. DELACROIX.

à Paris, le 16 Prairial, An 5
de la Republique Françaife, une
et indivisible.

(No. 2.)   Translation.

The Uundersigned Minister for Foreign Affairs of the French Republick, lost no Time in laying before the Executive Directory the Note which was transmitted to him on the 1st of June (O. S.) by Lord Grenville, in the Name of His Britannick Majesty. He is directed to answer it.

The Executive Directory sees with Satisfaction the Desire which the Cabinet of Saint James's expresses to put an End, at length, to the Calamities of War. It will receive with Eagerness the Overtures and

and Proposals which shall be made to it by the Court of England.

The Executive Directory desires notwithstanding, that the Negociations should be set on Foot at once for a Definitive Treaty. This Proceeding appears to the Directory preferable to a Congress, of which the Result must be remote; and which does not correspond with the ardent Desire that it has to re-establish, as quickly as possible, Peace between the Two Powers.

(Signed)   CH. DELACROIX.

Paris, 16 Prairial, 5th Year of the French Republick, one and indivisible.—(June 4, 1797).

(No. 3.)   Official Note.—Lord Grenville to the Minister for Foreign Affairs.

La Cour de Londres a reçu, avec la plus grande Satisfaction, les Assurances des Dispositions du Directoire Exécutif d'accueillir avec Empressement les Ouvertures pacifiques de la Grand Bretagne, aussi bien que de son Desir de rétablir, le plus promptement possible, la Paix entre les Deux Puissances.

Empressé d'y contribuer en tout ce qui peut dépendre de Lui, le Gouvernement Britannique ne tardera pas d'envoyer soit à Paris, soit à tel autre Lieu sur le Continent dont on pourra convenir, un Ministre pour traiter et conclure avec le Plénipotentiaire qui sera nommé par le Directoire Exécutif.

Le Soussigné est chargé de demander à connoitre le Voeu du Directoire sur le Lieu de la Négotiation, à fin qu'on puisse prendre ici une Détermination prompte à cet égard; et de prier le Ministre des Relations Extérieures de lui envoyer, sans Délai, les Passeports nécessaires pour que le Plénipotentiaire du Roi puisse se rendre au plutot à sa Destination. La Question de signer des Articles Preliminaires ou Définitifs dépendra nécessairement de la Marche et de la Tournure des Négotiations, aux-quelles, il sera

apporté

apporté de la Part de la Grande Bretagne, le Désir le plus sincère pour le prompt Rétablissement de la Paix.

(Signé) GRENVILLE.

à Westminster, ce 8 Juin 1797.

(No. 3.) Translation.

THE Court of London has received, with the greatest Satisfaction, the Assurances of the Dispositions of the Executive Directory to entertain with Eagerness the pacific Overtures of Great Britain, as well as of it's Desire to re-establish, as soon as possible, Peace between the Two Powers.

Anxious to contribute to it in every Thing which can depend upon itself, the British Government will not delay to send to Paris, or to such other Place, upon the Continent, as may be agreed upon, a Minister, to treat and conclude with the Plenipotentiary, who shall be appointed by the Executive Directory.

The Undersigned is directed to desire to know the Wish of the Directory, as to the Place of the Negotiation, in order that a speedy Determination may be taken here upon that Subject; and to request the Minister for Foreign Affairs to send him, without Delay, the necessary Passports, to enable the King's Plenipotentiary to repair immediately to his Destination. The Question of signing Preliminary or Definitive Articles, will necessarily depend upon the Progress and Turn of the Negotiations, to which, on the Part of Great Britain, will be brought the most sincere Desire for the speedy Re-establishment of Peace.

(Signed) GRENVILLE.

Westminster, June 8th, 1797.

(No. 4.) Official Note.—The Minister for Foreign Affairs to Lord Grenville.

Le Directoire Exécutif de la République Française a vu avec Satisfaction, par la Note Officielle du Lord Grenville, en Date du 8 Juin (v. st.) que la Cour de Londres se montrait disposée à entamer, sans Délai, la Négociation dont elle a fait récemment l'Ouverture. Rempli du même Empressement, convaincu que les Intentions du Gouvernement Britannique sont telles qu'il les annonce, Il à chargé le Ministre des Relations Extérieurs soussigné, de faire passer au Lord Grenville les Passeports nécessaires pour un Ministre chargé de pleins Pouvoirs à l'Effet de négocier et conclure un Traité de Paix définitif et séparé avec la République Française.

Le Directoire Exécutif à désigné la Commune de Lille pour le Point de Réunion des Plénipotentiaires respectifs.

(Signé) CH. DELACROIX.

à Paris, 23 Prairial,
An 5 de la Rep. Fr.

(No. 4.) Translation.

The Executive Directory of the French Republick has seen with Satisfaction, by the Official Note of Lord Grenville, dated June 8th (O. S.), that the Court of London shews itself disposed to set on Foot, without Delay, the Negotiation, for which It has lately made an Overture. Filled with the same Eagerness, convinced that the Intentions of the British Government are such as It describes them, the Directory has directed the Undersigned, Minister for Foreign Affairs, to transmit to Lord Grenville the necessary Passports for a Minister furnished with full Powers for the Purpose of negotiating a definitive and separate Treaty of Peace with the French Republick.

The

The Executive Directory has fixed upon the Commune of Lisle as the Place of Meeting for the respective Plenipotentiaries.

(Signed)   CH. DELACROIX.

à Paris, 23 Prairial, 5th Year
of the French Republick.
(June 11, 1797.)

(No. 5.)   Form of Passport.

Liberté, Egalité.   Fraternité, Union.

Au Nom de la Republique Française.

A TOUS Officiers Civils et Militaires, chargés de maintenir l'Ordre public dans les differens Departemens de la France, et de faire respecter le Nom François chez l'Etranger.

Laissés passer librement
chargé des pleins Pouvoirs de Sa Majesté Britannique, à l'effet de negocier, conclure, et signer un Traité de Paix Definitif et Separé avec la Republique Françaife, Natif de, &c. &c. &c.

allant à Lille, Departément du Nord, Lieu designé pour la Negotiation,
sans donner ni souffrir qu'il soit donné aucun Empêchement.

Le présent Passeport sera valable pour Decades seulement.

Donné à Paris, le 23 *Prairial*, l'An 5 de la Republique, Une et Indivisible.

Le Ministre des Relations Exterieures,

(Signé)   CH. DELACROIX.

Par le Ministre,

(Signé)   T. GUIRAUDET, Sec. Gen.

(No. 5.) Translation.

Liberty, Equality.   Fraternity, Union.

In the Name of the French Republick.

To all Officers, Civil and Military, charged to maintain public Order in the different Departments of France, and to make the French Name respected Abroad.

Allow to pass freely *furnished with the full Powers of His Britannick Majesty for the Purpose of negociating, concluding, and signing a Definitive and Separate Treaty of Peace with the French Republick, Native of, &c. &c. &c.*

going to Lille, Department of the North, the Place appointed for the Negotiation, without giving or suffering any Hindrance to be given to him.

This Passport shall be in force for   Decades only.

Given at Paris the 23 *Prairial*, 5th Year of the Republick, One and Indivisible.

The Minister Foreign Affairs,

    (Signed)   CH. DELACROIX.

By the Minister,

    (Signed)   T. GUIRAUDET.

(No. 6.)   Official Note.—Lord Grenville to the Minister for Foreign Affairs.

LE Soussigné a reçu de la Part du Ministre des Relations Extérieures de la République Françaife sa Note Officielle, avec le Passeporte qui y etoit joint.

La Cour de Londres accepte volontiers la Proposition du Gouvernement François par rapport au Lieu de la Négotiation, et consente à ce que Lille soit désigné pour la Reunion des Plénipotentiaries respectifs : Bien entendu que celui du Roi aura la Faculté d'expédier ses Couriers en droiture de Lille à Douvres

par

par Calais; et que les Batimens Anglais, désignés pour maintenir cette Communication, pourront entrer et fortir librement du Port de Calais, et naviguer en toute Sureté entre cette Ville et Douvres.

Au fujet de Paſſeport, le Souſſigné ſe voit obligé de remarquer que les Termes dans leſquels cet Inſtrument eſt redigé s'écartent de la Forme uſitée, par la Déſignation particuliere, qui s'y trouve, de la Nature et de l'étendue des Pouvoirs, et de la Miſſion du Plénipotentiaire du Roi.

Cette nouvelle Forme paroit ſuſceptible d'entrainer ſouvent de grands Inconveniens, et, d'après les Termes dont on s'eſt ſervi dans le Cas actuel, elle auroit celui de ne pas repondre avec Exactitude aux Pouvoirs et à la Miſſion du Miniſtre dont il eſt queſtion.

Ses Plein-Pouvoirs, redigés dans la Forme ordinaire, embraſſeroient tous les Cas; et en ne lui preſcrivant aucune Voie de Négotiation, lui donneroient la Faculté la plus illimitée de conclure des Articles ou des Traités, ſoit Preliminaires ſoit Definitifs, ſelon que cela pourra le mieux convenir au prompt Retabliſſement de la Paix, ſeul Objet de ſa Miſſion.

Mais la Cour de Londres ne tient nullement à la Concluſion d'un Traité Preliminaire, et ne donneroit la Preference qu'à tel Moyen, quelqu'il puiſſe être, qui ſera trouvé le plus propre à accélérer la Concluſion de la Paix.

Le Plénipotentiaire du Roi ſera donc egalement prêt, et autorizé à entrer ſans Délai en Négotiation, ſur l'un ou l'autre pied; ſur celui d'un Traité Préliminaire, ou bien, ſi cela continue à être le Voeu du Directoire, d'un Traité Définitif.

Pour ce qui regarde la Queſtion d'un Traité Separé;—il n'y auroit aucune Objection à terminer par un pareil Traité ce qui regarde les Intérêts reſpectifs de la France et de la Grande Bretagne; ſelon que cela s'eſt ordinairément pratiqué en pareil Cas: Mais le Roi ne peut laiſſer aucun Doute ſur Son Intention de pourvoir à ce qui eſt dû aux Intérêts de Son Allié la Reine Trés Fidelle. Et par une suite des mêmes Principes, Sa Majesté ne refusera pas d'entrer en telles Explication par rapport aux Interéts de l'Espagne et de la Hollande, qui pourroient parôitre nécessaires au Rétablissement de la Paix.

Après cette Explication franche et précise, le Gouvernement Britannique se persuade que le Directoire ne tardera pas de Lui faire parvenir un Passeport pour le Plénipotentiaire Britannique et sa Suite, dans la Forme usitée, et tel qu'il a été envoyé au Mois d'Octobre dernier pour la Mission dont Lord Malmesbury etoit chargé alors.

Dans cette Attente, et pour eviter tout Délai, Sa Majesté a déjà fait Choix du même Ministre pour La representer dans cette Occasion importante :—Et le Soussigné est chargé de demander à quel Jour le Plenipotentiaire Français pourra étre rendu à Lille ;—à fin que le Lord Malmsbury puisse y arriver à la même Epoque.

(Signé)   GRENVILLE.

à Westminster, ce 17 Juin 1797.

(No. 6.)   Translation.

THE Undersigned has received from the Minister for Foreign Affairs of the French Republick his Official Note, with the Passport which accompanied it.

The Court of London willingly accepts the Proposal of the French Government with respect to the Place of Negotiation, and consents that Lisle shall be appointed as the Place of Meeting for the respective Plenipotentiaries :—It being always understood, that the King's Plenipotentiary shall have Liberty to dispatch his Couriers directly from Lisle to Dover, by Way of Calais, and that the English Vessels, appointed for keeping up this Communication, shall be allowed freely to go into, and come out of, the Port of Calais, and to pass in perfect Safety between that City and Dover.

With

With respect to the Passport, the Undersigned finds himself under the Necessity of remarking that the Terms in which this Instrument is drawn up, differ from the usual Form, by the particular Description, which is inserted in them, of the Nature and Extent of the Powers, and of the Mission of the King's Plenipotentiary.

'This new Form appears liable to produce, in many Instances, considerable Inconveniences; and, according to the Terms used in this particular Instance, it would have the Disadvantage of not answering exactly to the Powers and the Mission of the Minister in question.

His full Powers, drawn up in the usual Form, will include every Case; and without prescribing to him any particular Mode of Negotiation, will give him the most unlimited Authority to conclude any Articles or Treaties, whether Preliminary or Definitive, as might best conduce to the speedy Re-establishment of Peace, which is the sole Object of his Mission.

But the Court of London does not by any Means make a Point of concluding a Preliminary Treaty, and would prefer only that Mode, whatever it may be, which shall be found the best calculated to accelerate the Conclusion of Peace.

The King's Plenipotentiary then will be equally ready, and authorized to begin the Negotiation without Delay, upon either footing; upon the footing of a Preliminary Treaty—or, should such continue to be the Wish of the Directory, upon that of a Definitive Treaty.

As to what regards the Question of a separate Treaty—there would be no Objection to settling, by a Treaty of this Kind, whatever relates to the respective Interests of France and of Great Britain, as has been usually the Practice in similar Cases: But the King can not allow any Doubt to subsist as to His Intention of providing for what is due to the Interests of His Ally Her Most Faithful Majesty. And in pur-

purfuance of the fame Principles, His Majefty will not refufe to enter into fuch Explanations with refpect to the Interefts of Spain and Holland as may appear neceffary for the Re-eftablifhment of Peace.

After this frank and precife Explanation, the Britifh Government is perfuaded that the Directory will not delay to tranfmit to them a Pafiport for the Britifh Plenipotentiary and his Suite, in the ufual Form, and fuch as was fent in the Month of October laft for the Miffion with with Lord Malmefbury was then charged.

In this Expectation, and <u>for the Sake of avoiding all Delay</u>, His Majefty has already made Choice of the fame Minifter to reprefent Him on this important Occafion. And the Underfigned is charged to enquire on what Day the French Plenipotentiary will be at Lifle, in order that Lord Malmefbury may arrive there at the fame Time.

(Signed)   GRENVILLE.

Weftminfter, June 17, 1797.

(No. 7.)   Official Note.—The Minifter for Foreign Affairs to Lord Grenville.

LE Souffigné Miniftre de Relations Extérieures a mis, auffitôt fa Reception, fous les yeux du Directoire Exécutif, la Note Officielle que lui a adreffée le Lord Grenville, en Date du 17 Juin 1797 (v. ft.). Il s'empreffe d'y repondre conformément aux Ordres qu'il a reçus.

Le Directoire, partageant bien fincèrement les Sentimens pacifiques que témoigne Sa Majefté Britannique, et voulant amener le plus promptement poffible Negotiations a une heureufe Iffue, perfifte a demander que les Negociateurs refpectifs s'occupent, auffitôt leur Réunion, d'un Traité Définitif. Il accepte avec Satisfaction le Confentement da Sa Majefté Britannique à cet égard, exprimé dans la Note du Lord Grenville.

Le

Le Directoire consent à ce que Sa Majesté Britannique fasse, par Son Plénipotentiaire, les propositions ou Stipulations, qu'il jugera convenables, pour Sa Majesté Trés Fidéle; comme reciproquement les Plénipotentiaires de la République en feront pour ses Alliés Sa Majesté Catholique et la République Batave.

Le Directoire consent à ce que la Négociation soit ouverte avec le Lord Malmesbury; cependant un autre Choix Lui eut paru d'un plus heureux Augure pour la prompte Conclusion de la Paix.

Le Directoire demande qu'il soit etabli en Principe, que chaque Paquebot Anglais, qui aura transporté le Plenipotentiaire ou un Courrier, repartira sur le Champ et ne pourra séjourner. Il donera des Ordres pour qu'il soit fourni sans Délai un Paquebot Français à chacun des Courriers, que le Plénipotentiaire de Sa Majesté Britannique expédiera. Il desire toutefois que les Courriers ne soient pas trop multipliés; leur Multiplication ayant été une des principales Causes de la Rupture des Negociations précédentes.

D'après les explacations ci-dessus, il devient inutile de transmettre au Lord Grenville un nouveau Passeport; les Restrictions, qu'il craignoit de voir dans celui qui lui a été adressé, se trouvant entièrement levées.

Les Plénipotentiaires Français seront rendus à Lille à l'Epoque où le Lord Malmesbury pourra y etre rendu lui-meme.

(Signé) CH. DELACROIX.

Paris, le 2 Messidor.

(No. 7.) Translation.

THE undersigned Minister for Foreign Affairs has laid before the Directory, immediately upon its Receipt, the Official Note addressed to him by Lord Grenville, dated June 17, 1797 (O. S.) He loses no Time in replying to it, according to the Orders which he has received.

The Directory, partaking most sincerely in the pacific Sentiments which His Britannick Majesty announces, and wishing to bring the Negotiations as quickly as possible to a happy issue, persists in requiring that the respective Plenipotentiaries shall begin immediately upon their Meeting to treat of a Definitive Treaty. The Directory accepts, with Satisfaction, the Consent of His Britannick Majesty upon this Subject, expressed in the Note of Lord Grenville,

The Directory consents that His Britannick Majesty shall make, by His Plenipotentiary, such Proposals or Stipulations as He shall think proper for Her Most Faithful Majesty, as in return the Plenipotentiaries of the Republick will do for their Allies his Catholic Majesty and the Batavian Republick.

The Directory consents that the Negotiation shall be opened with Lord Malmesbury. Another Choice would, however, have appeared to the Directory to augur more favourably for the speedy Conclusion of Peace. The Directory requires that it shall be established as a Principle, that each English Packet Boat, which shall have brought over either the Plenipotentiary or a Courier, shall return without Delay, and shall not be allowed to make any Stay. The Directory will give Orders that a French Packet Boat shall be furnished, without Delay, to each of the Couriers whom the Plenipotentiary of His Britannick Majesty shall dispatch. The Directory desires, at the same Time, that the Couriers should not be sent too frequently; the frequent sending of them having been one of the principal Causes of the Rupture of the former Negotiation.

After the above Explanation, it becomes unnecessary to transmit to Lord Grenville a new Passport;

the

the Restrictions which he apprehended were to be found in that which has been addressed to him, being entirely done away.

The French Plenipotentiaries will have arrived at Lisle by the Time at which Lord Malmesbury can himself be there.

(Signed)   CH. DELACROIX.

Paris, 2 Messidor. (June 20, 1797.)

(No. 8.)   Official Note.—Lord Grenville to the Minister for Foreign Affairs.

Le Soussigné a mis sous les yeux du Roi la Note Officielle du Gouvernement François qu'il a reçu le 23 du Mois courant.

Sur les Deux premiers Articles de cette Note les Deux Parties sont d'accord. Il n'y a donc rien à ajouter la dessus aux Explications précédentes; en conséquence desquelles Explications, le Lord Malmesbury procédera sans Délai à Lille, pour entrer en Négotiation avec les Plènipotentiaires François, pour la Confection d'un Traité Définitif. La Remarque du Directoire sur le Choix que Sa Majesté a jugé à propos de faire de Son Plénipotentiaire n'etant certainement de Nature à exiger aucune Reponse.

Le Gouvernement Britannique consent à l'Arrangement proposé pour les Paquebots; pourvû qu'il soit fourni regulierement, et sans le moindre Délai un Paquebot François pour chaque Courier que le Plénipotentiaire Britannique se verra dans le cas d'expédier: L'Exercice de son Droit incontestable à cet égard ne devant et ne pouvant etre réglée que par sa Discretion seule, dans la vue d'amener la Nègotiation dont il est chargé à une prompte et heureuse fin.

Pour ce qui est de la Rupture de la dernière Negotiation, les Circonstances et les Motifs en sont connus à toute l'Europe; et ce n'est pas au Moment d'entamer une nouvelle Discussion pacifique, que le

gou-

gouvernement Britannique pense qu'il peut etre utile de les rappeller.

Le Lord Malmesbury partira de Londres le 30 ce Mois pour se rendre de suite à Calais; d'où il réglera son Départ selon la Notification qu'il y recevra du Jour où les Ministres François pourront être rendus à Lille.

     (Signé) GRENVILLE.
à Westminster, ce 26 Juin 1797.

(No. 8.)   Translation.

THE Undersigned has laid before the King the Official Note of the French Government, which he received the 23d of the present Month.

As to the Two first Articles of this Note both Parties are agreed. On this Point therefore there is nothing to be added to the Explanations already given; in consequence of which Explanations Lord Malmesbury will, without Delay, proceed to Lisle to enter into a Negotiation with the French Plenipotentiaries for the Completion of a Definitive Treaty. The Remark of the Directory upon the Choice which His Majesty has thought fit to make of His Plenipotentiary, being certainly of a Nature not to require an Answer.

The British Government agrees to the Arrangement proposed for the Packet Boats; provided that a French Packet Boat shall be furnished regularly, and without the least Delay, for each Courier which the British Plenipotentiary shall find it necessary to dispatch: The Exercise of his incontestable Right in this Respect being to be governed by his own Discretion only, with a View to bringing the Negotiation with which he is charged to a speedy and successful End.

With regard to the Rupture of the last Negotiation, the Circumstances and the Motives of it are known to all Europe; and it is not at the Moment of entering into a new pacific Discussion that the
              British

British Government conceive it can be of no Use to recall them to Recollection.

Lord Malmesbury will set out for London on the 30th of this Month to proceed to Calais; from whence he will arrange his Departure according to the Notification he may receive of the Day on which the French Ministers may reach Lisle.

    (Signed) GRENVILLE.

Westminster, June 26th, 1797.

(No. 9.) Official Note.—The Minister for Foreign Affairs to Lord Grenville.

Le Ministre des Relations Exterieures soussigné, s'est empressé de mettre sous les yeux du Directoire Executif la Note Officielle, que lui à addressée le Lord Grenville, en Date du 26 Juin (v. st.) huit Messidor present Mois. En reponse à cette Note il a l'Honneur de déclarer au Lord Grenville que les Plenipotentiaires chargés par le Directoire de la Négotiation sont dèja réunis a Lille, et que les Conférences pourront être entamées, aussitôt que le Plenipotentiaire de Sa Majesté Britannique y sera rendu. Il à été pourvû à ce que les Paquebots ne manquassent jamais aux Courriers qu'il jugera à propos d'expedier à Londres.

Le Soussigné previent également le Lord Grenville qu'une Copie de la presente Note sera remise au Lord Malmesbury, à son Arrivèe à Calais, à fin que rien ne s'oppose à son Dèpart immèdiat pour Lille.

    (Signé) CH. DELACROIX.

a Paris, le 11 Messidor, An. 5.

(Note 9.)   Translation.

The undersigned Minister for Foreign Affairs lost no Time in laying before the Executive Directory the Official Note addressed to him by Lord Grenville, deted the 21st June (O. S.) 8th of the present Month Messidor.

In Answer to this Note, he has the Honor to declare to Lord Grenville, that the Plenipotentiaries charged by the Directory with the Negotiation, are already assembled at Lisle, and that the Conferences may be set on Foot as soon as the Plenipotentiary of His Britannick Majesty shall have arrived there. Provision has been made that there shall never be a Want of Packet Boats for the Couriers which he shall think proper to send to London.

The Undersigned at the same Time apprizes Lord Grenville, that a Copy of this Note will be delivered to Lord Malmesbury on his Arrival at Calais, in order that there may be nothing to hinder his immediate Departure for Lisle.

(Signed)   CH. DELACROIX.

Paris, 11th Messidor, 5th Year.
(June 29. 1797.)

(No. 10.)   Extract of a Dispatch from Lord Malmesbury to Lord Grenville, dated Lisle, July 6th, Thursday, 8 P. M. 1797.

My Lord,

HAVING had this Morning my first Conference with the French Plenipotentiaries, and having mutually exchanged our full Powers, I think it my Duty to dispatch a Messenger, in order that his Majesty may have the earliest Information of this Circumstance. My Dispatch however must be confined to this alone, as nothing whatever has yet passed relative to the Negotiation itself.

(No. 11.)   Copy of the full Powers of the French Plenipotentiaries.

Egalité.   *Liberté.*

Extrait des Regiſtres des Deliberations du Directoire Exécutif.

Paris, le Trente Prairial, l'an cinq de la Republique Françoise, Une et Indivisible.

LE Directoire Exécutif, après avoir oui le Rapport du Ministre des Relations Exterieures, arrête ce qui suit.

Les

Les Citoyens Letourneur, ci-devant Membre du Directoire Exécutif, Pleville le Pelley, et Maret, font autorifés à négocier avec le Miniftre Plenipotentiaire de Sa Majefté Britannique le Traité de Paix à conclure entre la Republique Françaife et la Grande Bretagne. Le Directoire leur donne les Plein-pouvoirs neceffaires pour arrêter et figner les Articles du Traité à intervenir. Ils fe conformeront aux Inftructions qui leur ont été, ou leur feront, données par le Directoire Exécutif, auquel ils rendront Comte des Progrés et de l'Iffue des Négociations.

Ils font egalement autorifés, et fous les mêmes Conditions, à ftipuler pour les Alliés de la Republique, Sa Majefté Catholique et la Republique Batave.

Le Citoyen Colchen, nommé Secretaire Général de la Legation Françaife, eft autorifé à affifter aux Conferences pour donner les Renfeignemens qui lui feront démandés, et prendre Note de ce qui fera convenu et arrêté.

Le prefent Arrêté ne fera imprimé quant à prefent.
Pour Expedition conforme,
De Prefident du Directoire Executif,
CARNOT.
Par le Directoire Executif de Secretaire Général,
LAGARDE.

(No. 11.)   Tranflation.

Liberty.   *Equality.*

Extract from the Regifters of the Deliberations of the Executive Directory.

> Paris the 30th Prairial, 5th Year of the French Republick, One and Indivifible.

THE Executive Directory, after having heard the Report of the Minifter for Foreign Affairs, decrees is follows:

The Citizens Letourneur, heretofore Member of he Executive Directory, Pleville le Pelley, and
Maret,

Maret, are authorized to negotiate with the Minister Plenipotentiary of His Britannick Majesty, the Treaty of Peace to be concluded between the French Republick and Great Britain. The Directory gives them the necessary full Powers for agreeing upon and signing the Articles of the Treaty to be made. They shall conform themselves to the Instructions which have been, or shall be, given to them by the Executive Directory, to whom they shall render an Account of the Progress and the Issue of the Negotiation.

They are equally authorized, and under the same Conditions, to stipulate for the Allies of the Republick, His Catholick Majesty and the Batavian Republick.

The Citizen Colchen, appointed Secretary General to the French Legation, is authorized to assist at the Conferences, to afford the Information which shall be required of him, and to take a Note of what shall be agreed upon and settled.

The present Decree shall not be printed for the present.

 A true Copy,
  The President of the Executive Directory,
       CARNOT.

  By the Executive Directory,
    the Secretary General,
       LAGARDE.

(No. 12.) Extracts of a Dispatch from Lord Malmsbury to Lord Grenville, dated Lisle, July 11, 1797.

I HAD the Honor in my last, by Brooks, of the 6th instant, to inform your Lordship of my Arrival here, of the Manner in which I had been received and of my having, in the usual Form, exchanged my full Powers with the French Plenipotentiaries.

On Friday the 7th at Noon we held our Second Conference.

         I opened

I opened this Second Conference with the French Plenipotentiaries, by saying, that I myself had no Observations to make on their full Powers, which appeared to be conformable to those usually given by the Directory to their Plenipotentiaries, and of course must be considered as sufficient for the Purposes expressed in them; that I, however, had transmitted them by a Messenger to my Court, and reserved to myself the Right of communicating any Objections or Remarks which I might receive by the Return of my Messenger, relative to them.

M. le Tourneur, to which, as President of the Commission, I addressed myself, replied, that they had taken precisely the same Steps as myself; that *they* considered the full Powers I had given in, as in due Form, and sufficient; but that they also reserved to themselves the same Right, in regard to Instructions they might receive from the Directory on this Subject, as I had claimed in regard to my Court.

To this, of course, I assented.

On Saturday the 8th instant I gave in the *Projet* precisely as I had received it from your Lordship; a Copy of which (A), as it is translated into French, I think it my Duty to inclose.

One of the French Plenipotentiaries proposed that some Time should be given them to take the Proposals I had made into Consideration, and begged of me merely for the Sake of Accuracy, and to help their Memory, that I would be good enough either to let M. Colchen put down on Paper, or myself send them a Note containing the Words with which I wished the Articles left in Blank to be filled up. I readily acquiesced in the latter Mode, and immediately on my Return sent them the inclosed Note (B).

On Sunday Evening I received the inclosed Note (C) from the French Plenipotentiaries, and in consequence of it went to the proposed Conference Yesterday.

One

One of the French Plenipotentiaries informed me on the Subject of the Projet I had given them, and the Note with which I had accompanied it, that as these Papers contain many Points on which their Instructions did not enable them to answer, they had, after having given them a very serious Attention, sent them, with such Observations as they had thought it their Duty to make on them, to the Directory, and that the Moment they received an Answer, they would communicate it to me. But that in the meanwhile, not to delay the Progress of the Negotiation, they wished that several Points which he termed insulated, but which, though not referred to in our Projet, were, he said, inseparably connected with the general Subject of Peace, might be discussed and got rid of now if I had no Objection, and that it was with this View they had requested me to meet them.—On my not expressing any Disapprobation to this Mode of Proceeding, *One of the French Plenipotentaries* began, by saying, that in the Preamble of the Treaty the Title of <u>King of France</u> was used; that this Title they contended could no longer be insisted on, the Abolition of it was in a Manner essential to the full Acknowledgment of the French Republick, and that as it was merely titular, as far as related to His Majesty, but quite otherwise in the Sense in which it applied to them, he hoped it would not be considered as an important Concession.

I informed him, that on all former Occasions a separate Article had been agreed to, which appeared to me to answer every Purpose they required, and which it was my Intention, as the Treaty advanced, to have proposed, as proper to make Part of this. The Article (the First of the separate ones in the Treaty of 1783) was then read; but they objected to it, as not fully meeting their Views. It was to the <u>Title itself</u>, as well as to any Right which might be supposed to arise from it, that they objected. I could scarce allow myself to treat this mode of reasoning

soning seriously. I endeavoured to make them feel that it was cavilling for a mere word; that it was creating Difficulties where none existed; and that if all the French Monarchs in the Course of Three Centuries had allowed this to stand in the Preamble of all Treaties and Transactions between the Two Countries, I could not conceive, after its having been used for so long a Period without any Claim or Pretention being set forth in consequence of it, how it could now affect either the Dignity, Security, or Importance of the Republick—that in Fact such Titles have ever been considered as indefeasable, and as Memorials and Records of former Greatness, and not as Pretensions to present Power—and I quoted the Titles of the Kings of Sardinia and Naples, &c. as Examples exactly in point. I argued however in vain. They treated it very gravely, and made so strong a Stand upon it, that I could not avoid taking it for Reference, which I thought it better to do, than feeling as I did at the Moment, to push the Conversation farther.

The Second insulated Point was a very material one indeed, and which, although it has been adverted to as a Proposal that might possibly be brought forward, I confess came upon me unexpectedly.—It was to ask either a Restitution of the Ships taken and destroyed at Toulon, or an Equivalent for them. They grounded this Claim on the Preliminary Declaration made by Lord Hood on his taking Possession of Toulon; and on the Eighth Article of the Declaration of the Committee of the Sections to him. They said, Peace they hoped was about to be re-established; that His Majesty, in acknowledging the Republic, admitted that a Sovereignty existed in the French Government; and of course that the Ships, held only a as Deposit by England till this legal Authority was admitted, ought now to be restored. I replied that this Claim was so perfectly unlooked for, that it was impossible for me to have been provided for it in my Instructions, and that I could therefore only convey my own private Sentiments on it, which were, that they could not have devised a Step more likely to defeat the great End of our Mission. *One of the French Plenipotentaries* said, that he sincerely hoped not; that without a Restitution of the Ships, an Equivalent might be found to effect the Purpose desired, since their great Object was, that something should appear to prove that this just Demand had not been overlooked by them, and was not left unsatisfied by us. I told him fairly, I did not see where this Equivalent was to be found, or how it could be appreciated; and that considering the great Advantages France had already obtained by the War, and those she was likely to obtain from the Act of Condescension I had already intimated His Majesty was disposed to make in order to restore Peace, I was much surprized, and deeply concerned at what I heard. I trusted, therefore, that this very inadmissible Proposal would be withdrawn. They said it was not in their Power; and *One of them*, from a written Paper before him, which he said were his Instructions, read to me Words to the Effect I have already stated.

Their Third Question was as to any Mortgage we might have upon the Low Countries, in consequence of Money lent to the Emperor by Great Britain— They wished to know if any such existed, since as they had taken the Low Countries charged with all their Incumbrances, they were to declare that they should not consider themselves bound to answer any Mortgage given for Money lent to the Emperor, for the Purpose of carrying on War against them.

I told them, that without replying to this Question, supposing the Case to exist, the Exception they required should have been stated in their Treaty with the Emperor, and could not at all be mixed up in ours; that if they had taken the Low Countries as they stood charged with *all* their Incumbrances, there could be no Doubt what these Words meant, and that

that if no Exception was stated in the First Instance none could be made with a retro-active Effect.

The French Plenipotentiaries, however, were as tenacious on this Point as on the other Two; and as I found to every Argument I used that they constantly opposed their Instructions, I had nothing to do but to desire that they would give me a written Paper stating their Three Claims, in order that I might immediately transmit it to your Lordship, and on this being promised, our Conference broke up

Between Four and Five P. M. Yesterday, I received the enclosed Note (D), and I have lost no Time since it is in my Possession in preparing to send away a Messenger, as independent of the disagreeable Subjects brought forward in this last Conference, and which it is material should be communicated without Delay. I am anxious His Majesty should be informed of what has passed in general up to this day, as it may perhaps furnish some Ideas as to the possible Event of the Negotiation.

COPY of the PROJET.

(No. 13. A.)   Projet delivered by Lord Malmesbury to the French Plenipotentiaries in their Conference, July 8th, 1797.

Projet d'un Traité de Paix.

SOIT notoire a tous ceux qu'il appartiendra ou peut appartenir en Maniere quelconque. Le Sereniffime et trés puissant Prince George Trois, par la Grace de Dieu, Roi de la Grande Bretagne, de France, et d'Irlande, Duc de Bronsvic et de Lunebourg, Archi Treforier et Electeur du Saint Empire Romain, &c. et le Directoire Exécutif de la Republique Françaife, defirant également de faire cesser la

E   Guerre

Guerre qui exifte depuis quelque Tems entre leurs Etats refpectifs, ont nommé et conftitué pour leurs Plénipotentiaires, chargés de conclure et figner le Traité de Paix Définitif; fcavoir, Sa Majefté le Roi de la Grande Bretagne, le Lord Baron de Malmefbury, Pair du Royaume de la Grande Bretagne, Chevalier du tres Honorable Ordre du Bain, Confeiller Privé Actuel de Sa Majefté, et le Directoire Exécutif de la République Françoife

lefquels après avoir échangé leurs Pleinpouvoirs refpectifs, font convenus des Articles fuivans :

I. Auffitot que ce Traité fera figné et ratifié, il y aura une Paix univerfelle et perpétuelle, tant par Mer que par Terre, et une Amitié fincere et conftante entre les Deux Parties Contractantes, leurs états, Territoires, et Peuples, fans Exception de Lieux ni de Perfonnes, en forte que les Hautes Parties Contractantes apporteront la plus grande Attention à maintenir entre Elles, leurs dits états, Territoires, et Peuples, cette Amitie et Correfpondance reciproque, fans permettre dorénavant, que de Part ni d'autre, on commette aucune Sorte d'Hoftilités, par Mer ou par Terre, pour quelque Caufe, ou fous quelque Pretexte que ce puiffe être. Il y aura un Oubli et Amniftie generale de tout ce qui a pû être fait ou commis de Part ou d'autre avant ou depuis le Commencement de la Guerre ; et on evitera foigneufment tout ce qui pourroit altérer à l'avenir l'Union heureufement rétablie.

D'abord après l'échange des Ratifications de ce Traité, on expédiera des Ordres, tant aux Armées qu'aux Efcadres des deux Parties, de fair ceffer toutes. Hoftilities ; et à fin d'affurer l'Exécution de cet Article, on accordera de part et d'autre des Paffeports de Mer aux Vaiffeaux chargés de porter la Nouvelle de la Paix aux Poffeffions des Deux Parties.

II. Les Traités de Paix de Nimegue de 1678 et 1679, de Ryfwick de 1697, et d'Utrecht de 1713 ;

celui

celui de Bade de 1714; celui de la Triple Alliance de la Haye de 1717; celui de la Quadruple Alliance de Londres de 1718; le Traité de Paix de Vienne de 1738; le Traité Definitif d'Aix la Chapelle de 1748; le Traité Definitif de Paris de 1763; et celui de Versailles de 1783, fervent de Bafe et de Fondement à la Paix, et au prefent Traité. Et pour cet Effet ils font tous renouvellés et confirmés dans la meilleure Forme, en forte qu'ils devront être obfervés exactement à l'avenir dans toute leur Teneur, et religieufement exécutés de Part et d'autre, dans tous les Points auxquels il n'eft pas dérogé par le prefent Traité de Paix.

III. Tous les Prifonniers faits de part et d'autre, tant par Terre que par Mer, et les Otages ou levés ou donnés pendant la Guerre, feront reftitués, fans Rançon, dans Six Semaines au plus tard, à compter du Jour de l'échange de la Ratification du prefent Traité. Chaque Partie foldant refpectivement les Avances qui auront été faites pour la Subfiftance et l'Entretien de fes Prifonniers dans les Pais où ils auront été detenus, conformément aux Reçus et états conftatés, et autres Titres autentiques, qui feront fournis de Part et d'autre; et il fera donné reciproquement des Suretés pour le Payement des Dettes que les Prifonniers auroient pû contracter dans les Etats ou ils auroient été detenus, jufqu' à leur entiere Liberté.

IV. A l'egard du Droit de Pêche fur les Côtes de L'Ifle de Terre Neuve, et des Ifles adjacentes, et dans le Golf St. Laurent, les Deux Parties feront remifes dans la même Situation où Elles fe trouvoient refpectivement d'après les Traités et Engagemens fubfiftans à l'Epoque du Commencement de la Guerre. Et dans cette Vue, Sa Majefté confent de reftituer à la France en toute Proprieté les Ifles de St. Pierre et Miquelon.

V. Le même Principe du *Status ante Bellum* eft adopté du Confentement actuel des Deux Parties, à

l'egard

l'egard de toutes leurs Poſſeſſions et Droits reſpectifs dans toutes les Parties du Monde; ſauf les Exceptions qui ſeront ſtipulées par les Articles ſuivants du Traité actuel. Et dans cette Intention toutes les Poſſeſſions ou Territoires que l'une des Parties Contractantes pourroit avoir conquis ou pourroit conquérir ſur l'autre (et qui ne ſeront pas ſpécialement exceptés dans ce Traité), ſeront rendus à celle des Deux Parties a qui ils appartenoient au Commencement de la Guerre actuelle.

VI. Les Deux Parties ſont convenus d'excepter de ce Principe de Reſtitution reciproque

qui reſtera en toute Proprieté à Sa Majeſté Britannique.

VII. Dans tous les Cas de Reſtitution ſtipulés par le preſent Traité, les Forterreſſes ſeront rendues dans le même état où elles ſe trouvent actuellement, et il ne ſera fait aucun Dommage aux Ouvrages qui auront été conſtruits depuis leur Conquête.

VIII. Il eſt auſſi convenu, que dans chaque Cas de Reſtitution ou de Ceſſion ſtipulé par un Article quelconque du preſent Traité, il ſera accordé un Eſpace de Trois Ans, à dater de la Notification du Traité, dans l'Endroit ou Territoire reſpectivement reſtitué ou cédé, aux Perſonnes de quelque Deſcription que ce ſoit, Habitants du dit Endroit ou Territoire, ou Poſſeſſeurs de Proprietés en Vertu d'un Titre quelconque reconnu comme valable avant la Guerre, ou qui leur ſeront dévoluës depuis, d'après les Loix qui exiſtaient alors; durant lequel Eſpace de Trois Ans ils pourront reſter et demeurer dans le libre Exercice de leur Religion, et dans la Jouïſſance de leurs Poſſeſſions et Effèts aux mêmes Conditions et en vertu des mêmes Titres ſous leſquels ils en ſont devenus Poſſeſſeurs, ſans être expoſés en aucune Maniere, ni ſous aucune Pretexte, à être pourſuivis ou traduits en Juſtice à cauſe de leur Conduite paſſée, excepté pour la Decharge de Dettes juſtes et contractées envers des Particuliers; et que tous ceux qui dans l'Eſpace
de

de Mois après la Notification de ce Traité declareront au Gouvernement, qui sera alors établi, leur Intention de se retirer eux ou leurs Effets, et de se rendre ailleurs, auront et obtiendront sous le Délai d'Un Mois après telle Declaration, pleine Liberté de partir, et de retirer leurs Effets, ou de les vendre et aliéner tant leurs Biens meubles qu' immeubles, en tout Tems pendant le dit Espace de Trois Ans, sans Empêchement ou Contrainte, excepté à cause des Dettes qu'ils auront pû contracter, ou dans le Cas d'une Poursuite criminelle pour des Faits commis postérieurement à la Notification du présent Traité

IX. Comme il est necessaire d'assigner une Epoque pour les Restitutions cy dessus stipulées, il est convenu qu'elles auront Lieu en Europe dans l'Espace d'un Mois, en Afrique et en Amérique dans trois Mois, et en Asie dans Six Mois après la Ratification du présent Traité.

X. Pour empécher le Renouvellement des Procès qui ont été terminés dans les Territoires a restituer en vertu de ce Traité, il est convenu que les Jugemens rendus en dernier Ressort, sur les Procès entre Particuliers et qui ont acquis Force de Choses jugées, seront maintenus et executés suivant leur Forme et Teneur.

XI. La Decision des Prises et des Saisies de Vaisseaux avec leur Cargaisons pris en pleine Mer, ou arrêtés dans les Ports de l'union ou de l'autre Pays, antérieurement aux Hostilités, sera remise aux Cours de Justice respectives; de sorte que la Validité des dites Prises et Saisies sera décidée selon le Droit des Gens et les Traités dans les Cours de Justice de la Nation qui aura fait la Capture, ou commandé les Saisies. Et pour prevenir tous les Sujets de Plainte et de Contestation qui pourroient naître à l'Occasion des Prises qui pourroient être faites en Mer depuis la Signature du Traité actuel, on est convenu reciproquement que les Vaisseaux et Effets qui pourroient être

être pris dans la Manche ou Mer Britannique et dans les Mers du Nord, après l'Efpace de Douze Jours, à compter depuis l'échange des Ratifications de ce Traité, feront de Part et d'autre reftitués :—Que le Terme fera d'un Mois depuis la Manche ou Mer Britannique et les Mers du Nord, jufqu' aux Ifles Canaries inclufivement, foit dans l'Ocean, foit dans la Méditerranée :—De Deux Mois depuis les dites Ifles Canaries jufqu' à la Ligne Equinoctiale ou l'Equateur :—De Trois Mois depuis l'Equateur en comprenant tout ce qui eft fitue a l'Oueft du Cap de Bonne Efperance, et à l'Eft du Cap de Horn :—Et enfin, de Cinq Mois dans tous les autres Endroits du Monde, fans aucune Exception ni autre Diftinction plus particuliere de Tems et de Lieu.

XII. Les Alliés des Deux Parties contractantes, fcavoir, Sa Majefté Trés Fidelle comme Allié de Sa Majefté Britannique, et Sa Majefté Catholique et la Republique Batave comme Alliés de la Republique Françaife, feront invités par les Deux Parties Contractantes à accéder à cette Paix aux Termes et Conditions fpecifiés dans les Trois Articles fuivans; dont les Deux Parties Contractantes fe garantiffent reciproquement l'Exécution, y etànt refpectivement autorifés par leurs fufdits Alliés :—Et les Deux Parties Contractantes font en outre convenues, que fi leurs Alliés refpectifs n'y auraient pas ainfi accédé dans l'Efpace de Deux Mois à compter de l'echange des Ratifications du prefent Traité, la Partie qui refufera fon Acceffion, ne recevra de fon Allié ni Aide ni Secours de telle Nature qui ce foit pendant la Durée alterieure de la Guerre.

XIII. Sa Majefté Britannique s'engage à conclure un Traité de Paix Definitif avec Sa Majefté Catholique fur le Pied du *Status ante Bellum*, avec l'Exception de

qui reftera en pleine Proprieté à Sa Majefté Britannique.

XIV. Sa

XIV. Sa Majesté Britannique s'engage pareillement à conclure un Traité de Paix Définitif avec la Republique Batave sur le Pied du *Status ante Bellum*, avec l'Exception de

qui restera en pleine Proprieté à Sa Majesté Britannique et de

qui sera cedé à Sa Majesté Britannique en Echange de.

En Consideration de ces Restitutions à faire par Sa Majesté Britannique, toute la Proprieté appartenante au Prince d'Orange, au Mois de Decembre 1794, et qui à été séquestrée saisie ou confisquée depuis cette Epoque, lui sera rendue, ou bien elle lui sera pleinement compensée par un Equivalent pécuniare. Et la Republique Française s'engage en outre à lui procurer à la Paix générale une Compensation équivalente de la Perte de ses Charges et Dignités dans les Provinces Unies; et les Personnes qui auront été emprisonnées ou exilées, ou dont les Propriétés auront été séquestrées, ou confisquées dans la dite République à Cause de leur Attachment ax Intérêts de la Maison d'Orange, ou à l'ancien Gouvernment des Provinces Unies, seront mises en Liberté, ou auront la Permission de retourner dans leur Patrie d'y resider, et d'y jouir de leurs Proprietès en se conformant aux Loix et à la Constitution qui y sont établies.

XV. La République Françoise s'engage à conclure un Traité de Paix Définitif avec Sa Majesté Tres Fidelle sur le Pied du *Status ante Bellum*, sans qu'aucune Demande ou Condition onéreuse soit exigée de Part ou d'autre.

XVI. Toutes les Stipulations contenues dans ce Traité, relatives au Tems et à la Maniere de faire les Restitutions c'y mentionnées, ainsi que tous les Privileges y reservés aux Habitants ou Proprietaires des Isles ou Territories restitués ou cedés, seront censés se rapporter egalement aux Restitutions à faire en vertu des Trois derniers Articles; scavoir, le

Treizieme,

Triezieme, Quatorzieme, et Quinzieme, hors les Cas où l'on pourrait y déroger du Consentement mutuel des Parties intéressées.

XVII. Tous les précédents Traités de Paix faits entre les Parties contractantes et leurs Alliés respectifs de Part et d'autre nommés dans les Trois susdits Articles, qui subsistaient et etaient en force avant le Commencement des Hostilités, seront respectivement renouvellés, excepté en tant qu'on pourra y déroger d'un Consentement mutuel; et les Articles de ce Traité qui regardent la Restitution des Prisonniers, la Cessation des Hostilités, et la Décision à l'egard des Prises et Saisies, se rapporteront également aux Parties respectives nommées dans les Trois susdits Articles, et seront censés être Obligatoires entre elles, aussitôt qu'elles auront respectivement et formellement accédé à ce Traité.

XVIII. Toutes les Sequestrations mises par aucune des Parties nommées dans ce Traité, sur les Droits, Proprietés, ou Dettes des Particuliers, appartenans à une autre des dites Parties, seront levées, et la Proprieté de toute Espece sera rendue en entier au Proprietaire légal, ou bien il lui en sera faite une juste Compensation : Et toutes Plaintes à cause de Dommages faits à la Proprieté des Individus d'une Maniere contraire aux Usages et Droits de la Guerre, et toutes Réclamations de Droits ou de Proprietés appartenans à des Particuliers aux Epoques du Commencement des Hostilités respectivement entre les dites Parties, scavoir, la Grande Bretagne et le Portugal d'un Coté, et la France, l'Espagne, et la Hollande, de l'autre; et que, selon les Usages reçus et les Loix des Nations, l'Epoque de la Paix devroit faire revivre, seront reçues, entendues, et jugées dans les Cours de Justice respectives des différentes Parties; et pleine Justice sera rendue par chacune des dites Parties aux Sujets et Peuples de l'autre, de la même Maniere qu'à ses propres Sujets et Peuples.

Et

Et en cas qu'il s'éleve des Plaintes sur l'Execution de cet Article, lesquelles ne pourront être satisfaites par un Arrangement mutuel entre les Gouvernemens respectifs dans l'Espace de Douze Mois après qu'elles leur auront été addressées, les dites Plaintes seront jugées par des Commissaires jurés que l'on nommera de Part et d'autre, avec Pouvoir de faire intervenir un Arbitre de quelque Nation neutre; et la Decision des dits Commissaires sera absolue, et sans Appel.

XIX. Sa Majesté Britannique et la République Françoise promettent d'observer sincérement, et de bonne Foi, tous les Articles contenus et établis dans le present Traité; et ne souffriront pas qu'il y soit fait de Contraventions se garantissent, generalement et réciproquement, toutes les Stipulations du present Traité.

XX. Les Ratifications solemnelles du present Traité, expediées en bonne et due Forme, seront echangées en   entre les Parties Contractanets, dans l'Espace d'un Mois, ou plutot s'il est possible, à compter du Jour de la Signature du présent Traité.

En Foi de quoi, &c. &c.

(No. 13. A.)   Translation.

Project of a Treaty of Peace.

Be it known to all those whom it shall or may in any manner concern. The most Serene and most Potent Prince George the Third, <u>by the Grace of God, King of Great Britain, France,</u> and Ireland, Duke of Brunswic and Lunenburgh, Arch Treasurer and Elector of the Holy Roman Empire, and the Executive Directory of the French Republick, being equally desirous to put an End to the War, which has for some Time past subsisted between the Dominions of the Two Parties, have named and constituted for their Plenipotentiaries, charged with the concluding and signing of the Definitive Treaty of Peace;

Peace; viz. the King of Great Britain, the Lord Baron of Malmesbury, a Peer of the Kingdom of Great Britain, Knight of the Most Honourable Order of the Bath, Privy Councillor to His Britannick Majesty, and the Executive Directory of the French Republic,

who, after having exchanged their respective full Powers, have agreed upon the following Articles:

I. As soon as this Treaty shall be signed and ratified, there shall be an universal and perpetual Peace as well by Sea as by Land, and a sincere and constant Friendship between the Two contracting Parties, and their Dominions, and Territories, and People, without Exception of either Places or Persons; so that the High Contracting Parties shall give the greatest Attention to the maintaining between themselves and their said Dominions, Territories, and People, this reciprocal Friendship and Intercourse, without permitting hereafter, on either Part, any Kind of Hostilities to be committed either by Sea or by Land, for any Cause, or under any Pretence whatsoever. There shall be a general Oblivion and Amnesty of every Thing which may have been done or committed by either Party towards the other before or since the Commencement of the War; and they shall carefully avoid for the future every Thing which might prejudice the Union happily re-established.

Immediately after the Exchange of the Ratifications of this Treaty, Orders shall be sent to the Armies and Squadrons of both Parties to stop all Hostilities; and for the Execution of this Article, Sea Passes shall be given on each Side to the Ships dispatched to carry the News of Peace to the Possessions of the Two Parties.

II. The Treaties of Peace of Nimeguen of 1678 and 1679, of Ryswick of 1697, and of Utrecht of 1713; that of Baden of 1714; that of the Triple Alliance of the Hague of 1717; that of the Quadruple Alliance of London of 1718; the Treaty of

Peace

Peace of Vienna of 1736; the Definitive Treaty of Aix la Chapelle of 1748; the Definitive Treaty of Paris of 1763; and that of Verſailles of 1783, ſerve as a Baſis and Foundation to the Peace, and to the preſent Treaty. And for this Purpoſe they are all renewed and confirmed in the beſt Form, ſo that they are to be exactly obſerved for the future in their full Tenour, and religiouſly executed by both Parties in all the Points which ſhall not be derogated from by the preſent Treaty of Peace.

III. All the Priſoners taken on either Side, as well by Land as by Sea, and the Hoſtages carried away or given during the War, ſhall be reſtored, without Ranſom, in Six Weeks at lateſt, to be computed from the Day of the Exchange of the Ratifications of the preſent Treaty.—Each Party reſpectively diſcharging the Advances which ſhall have been made for the Subſiſtence and Maintenance of their Priſoners in the Country where they ſhall have been detained, according to the Receipts, atteſted Accounts, and other authentic Vouchers, which ſhall be furniſhed on each Side; and Security ſhall be reciprocally given for the Payment of the Debts which the Priſoners may have contracted in the Countries where they may have been detained, until their entire Releaſe.

IV. With reſpect to the Rights of Fiſhery on the Coaſts of the Iſland of Newfoundland, and of the Iſlands adjacent, and in the Gulph of St. Lawrence, the Two Parties ſhall return to the ſame Situation in which they ſtood reſpectively, according to the Treaties and Engagements ſubſiſting at the Period of the Commencement of the War. And with this View, His Majeſty conſents <u>to reſtore to France</u>, in full Right, the <u>Iſlands of St. Pierre and Miquelon</u>.

V. The ſame Principle of the State of Poſſeſſion before the War, is adopted by mutual Conſent, with reſpect to all other Poſſeſſions and Rights on both Sides, in every Part of the World; ſave only the

Excep-

× This article is conditionally given up. See. N° 14. B.
p. 43 H

(36)

Exceptions which are stipulated by the subsequent Articles of this Treaty. And, to this Intent, all Possessions or Territories which have or may have been conquered by One of the Parties from the other (and not specially excepted in this Treaty), shall be restored to the Party to whom they belonged at the Commencement of the present War.

× VI. From this Principle of mutual Restitution, the Two Parties have agreed to except   which shall remain to His Britannick Majesty in full Sovereignty.

VII. In all the Cases of Restitution provided by the present Treaty, the Fortresses shall be restored in the same Condition in which they now are, and no Injury shall be done to any Works that have been constructed since the Conquest of them.

VIII. It is also agreed, that in every Case of Restitution or Cession provided by any of the Articles of this Treaty, the Term of Three Years from the Date of the Notification of the Treaty, in the respective Territory or Place restored or ceded, shall be allowed to Persons of whatever Description, residing or being in the said Territory or Place, possessed of Property therein under any Title existing before the War, or which has since devolved to them by the Laws then existing; during which Term of Three Years they shall remain and reside unmolested in the Exercise of their Religion, and in the Enjoyment of their Possessions and Effects, upon the Conditions and Titles under which they so acquired the same, without being liable in any Manner, or under any Pretence, to be prosecuted or sued for their past Conduct, except as to the Discharge of just Debts to Individuals; and that all those who, within the Time of   Months after the Notification of this Treaty, shall declare to the Government, then established, their Intention to withdraw themselves, or their Effects, and to remove to some other Place, shall have and ob-

tain

tain within One Month after such Declaration full Liberty to depart and to remove their Effects, or to sell and dispose of the same, whether moveable or immoveable, at any Time within the said Period of Three Years, without any Restraint or Hindrance, except on Account of Debts at any Time contracted, or of any criminal Prosecution for Acts done subsequent to the Notification of this Treaty.

IX. As it is necessary to appoint a certain Period for the Restitutions herein-before stipulated, it is agreed, that the same shall take place in Europe within (One Month), in Africa and America within (Three Months), and in Asia within (Six Months), after the Ratification of the present Treaty.

X. For preventing the Revival of the Law Suits which have been ended in the Territories to be restored by virtue of this Treaty, it is agreed, that the Judgements in private Causes pronounced in the last Resort, and which have acquired the Force of Matters determined, shall be confirmed and executed according to their Form and Tenour.

XI. The Decision of the Prizes and Seizures of Ships and their Cargoes taken at Sea or seized in the Ports of either Country, prior to the Hostilities, shall be referred to the respective Courts of Justice; so that the Legality of the said Prizes and Seizures shall be decided according to the Law of Nations, and to Treaties; in the Courts of Justice of the Nation which shall have made the Capture, or ordered the Seizures. And in order to prevent all Causes of Complaint and Dispute which may arise on account of Prizes which may be made at Sea after the Signing of this Treaty; it is reciprocally agreed that the Vessels and Effects which may be taken in the British Channel and in the North Seas, after the Space of Twelve Days, to be computed from the Exchange of the Ratifications of this Treaty, shall be restored on each Side:—That the Term shall be One Month from the British Channel and the North Seas, as far

as

as the Canary Iſlands, incluſively, whether in the Ocean, or in the Mediterranean: Two Months from the ſaid Canary Iſlands as far as the Equinoctial Line or Equator;—Three Months from the Equator to any Part to the Weſtward of the Cape of Good Hope, and the Eaſtward of Cape Horn:—And, laſtly, Five Months in all other Parts of the World, without any Exception or any more particular Deſcription of Time or Place.

XII. The Allies of the Two Parties, that is to ſay, Her Moſt Faithful Majeſty as Ally of His Britannick Majeſty, and His Catholick Majeſty and the Batavian Republick as Allies of the French Republick, ſhall be invited by the Two Contracting Parties to accede to this Peace on the Terms and Conditions ſpecified in the Three following Articles; the Execution of which the ſaid Two Contracting Parties reciprocally guarantee to each other, being thereto reſpectively authorized by their above-mentioned Allies:—And the Two Contracting Parties further agree, that if their Allies reſpectively ſhall not have ſo acceded within the Space of Two Months after the Exchange of the Ratifications of this Treaty, the Party ſo refuſing to accede, ſhall not receive from its Ally any Aid or Succour of any Nature during the further Continuance of the War.

XIII. His Britannick Majeſty engages to conclude a Definitive Peace with His Catholick Majeſty on the Footing of the State of Poſſeſſion before the War, with the Exception of *
which ſhall remain in full Sovereignty to His Britannick Majeſty.

XIV. His Britannick Majeſty in like Manner engages to conclude a Definitive Peace with the Batavian Republick on the ſame Footing of the State of Poſſeſſion before the War, with the Exception of x

which ſhall remain to His Britannick Majeſty in full Sove-

* *This Blank propoſed to be filled with* *the Iſld. of Trinidad. See p. 43* +

x *propoſed to be filled up with the Cape & Dutch Poſſsⁿ in Ceylon — ſee p. 44* X *proposed to be filled with Cochin — Negapatnam — see p. 44*

Sovereignty, and of ˣ   which
shall be ceded to His Majesty in Exchange for

In Consideration of these Restitutions, to be hereby made by His Britannick Majesty, all Property belonging to the Prince of Orange, in the Month of December 1794, and which has been seized and confiscated since that Period, shall be restored to him, or a full Equivalent for Money given him for the same. And the French Republick further engages to procure for him, at the general Peace, an adequate Compensation for the Loss of his Offices and Dignities in the United Provinces; and the Persons who have been imprisoned or banished, or whose Property has been sequestered or confiscated in the said Republick, on Account of their Attachment to the Interests of the House of Orange, or to the former Government of the United Provinces, shall be released, and shall be at Liberty to return to their Country, and to reside therein, and to enjoy their Property there, conforming themselves to the Laws and Constitution there established.

XV. The French Republick engages to conclude a Definitive Peace with Her Most Faithful Majesty, on the same Footing, of the State of Possession before the War, and without any further Demand or burthensome Condition being made on either Side.

XVI. All the Stipulations contained in this Treaty, respecting the Time and Manner of making the Restitutions therein mentioned, and all the Privileges thereby reserved to the Inhabitants or Proprietors in the Islands or Territories restored or ceded, shall apply in like Manner to the Restitutions to be made by virtue of any of the Three last Articles, viz. the XIIIth, XIVth, and XVth, except in those Instances where the same may be derogated from by the mutual Consent of the Parties concerned.

XVII. All former Treaties of Peace between the respective Parties, to whom the said Three Articles relate, and which subsisted and were in force at the

Com-

Commencement of Hostilities between them respectively, shall be renewed, except in such Instances only where the same may be derogated from by mutual Consent; and the Articles of this Treaty for the Restoration of Prisoners, the Cessation of Hostilities, and the Decision relative to Prizes and Seizures, shall equally apply to the respective Parties to whom the said Three Articles relate, and shall be held to be in full force between them, as soon as they shall respectively and in due form have acceded to this Treaty.

XVIII. All Sequestrations imposed by any of the Parties named in this Treaty, on the Rights, Properties, or Debts, of Individuals belonging to any other of the said Parties, shall be taken off, and the Property of whatever Kind shall be restored in the fullest Manner to the lawful Owner; or just Compensation be made for it: And all Complaints of Injury done to private property, contrary to the usual Practice and Rules of War, and all Claims of private rights or property which belonged to Individuals at the periods of the Commencement of Hostilities respectively, between the said parties, viz. Great Britain and Portugal on the one Side, and France, Spain, and Holland, on the other; and which ought, according to the usual practice and Laws of Nations, to revive at the period of peace, shall be received, heard, and decided, in the respective Courts of Justice of the different parties; and full Justice therein shall be done by each of the said parties to the Subjects and people of the other, in the same Manner as to their own Subjects or people.

And if any Complaint should arise respecting the Execution of this Article, which Complaints shall not be settled by mutual Agreement between the respective Governments within twelve Months after the same shall have been preferred to them, the same shall be determined by sworn Commissioners to be appointed on each Side, with Power to call in an Arbitrator

bitrator of any indifferent Nation; and the decifion of the said Commissioners shall be binding, and without Appeal.

XIX. His Britannick Majesty and the French Republick promise to observe sincerely, and bonâ fide, all the Articles contained and established in the present Treaty; and they will not suffer the same to be infringed, directly or indirectly, by their respective Subjects; and the said Contracting Parties guarantee to each other, generally and reciprocally, all the Stipulations of the present Treaty:

XX. The solemn Ratifications of the present Treaty, prepared in good and due Form, shall be exchanged in   between the Contracting Parties, in the Space of a Month, or sooner if possible, to be computed from the Day of the Signature of the Signature of the present Treaty.

In Witness whereof, &c. &c.

(No. 14. B.) Note from Lord Malmesbury to the French Plenipotentiaries.

Le Ministre Plénipotentiaire de Sa Majesté Britannique, pour satisfaire au Desir qu'ont témoigné à la Conférence de ce Matin les Ministres Plénipotentiaires de la République Française, a l'Honneur de leur adresser la Note suivante en les priant toutefois de la regarder moins comme une Pièce officielle, que comme une Communication confidentielle et verbale; et comme une Preuve de son Empressement à faciliter le Progrès de la Negociation, en leur offrant dès le premier pas, tous les Eclaircissements qui dépendent de lui sur le Projèt du Traité qu'il leur a remis.

Si, comme l'assurent les Ministres Plénipotentiaires de la République Française, il est contraire à leurs Instructions les plus positives d'entrer en aucune Discussion sur la Cession des Objets qui appartenaient à la France avant la Guerre, il est inutile de s'appuyer sur l'Article VI. puisque les Compensations que Sa Majesté

G

jefté Britannique aurait demandées par cet Article, en rétour des Reftitutions qu'elle eft difpofé à faire pour le Rétabliffement de la Paix, devront fe trouver d'après cette Déclaration, dans les Ceffions à faire, foit par Sa Majefté Catholique, foit par la République Batave.

C'eft pourquoi dans l'Article XIII. après les Mots *Status ante Bellum*, le Lord Malmefbury propofera d'inférer les Mots fuivants : " A l'Exception de l'Ifle " de Trinidad, qui reftera en toute Propriété à Sa " Majefté Britannique."

Le Lord Malmefbury croit qu'il eft peu neceffaire de répéter les Raifons qui l'engagent à infifter fur la Confervation de cette Conquête, à moins qu'elle ne foit compenfée par quelque autre Ceffion qui puiffe balancer le Surcroit de Puiffance refultante de l'Acquifition faite par la France de la Partie Efpagnole de St. Domingue.

Quant à l'Article XIV. le Lord Malmefbury propofe, qu'après les Mots *Status ante Bellum*, on ajoute : " Avec Exception de la Ville, du Fort, et de l'Eta-" bliffement du Cap de Bonne Efperance, et des Pof-" feffions qui ont appartenu aux Hollandois avant la " Guerre dans l'Ifle de Ceylon, et de la Ville et " Fort de Cochin, qui feront cédés à Sa Majefté " Britannique, en Echange de la Ville de Negapat-" nam, et de fes Dépendances."

Le Lord Malmfbury réitère aux Miniftres Plénipotentiaires de la Republique Françaife, le Témoignage de fon Empreffement à concourir avec eux, en tout ce qui dépend de lui, pour amener la Negociation à une heureufe Iffuë; et les prie en même Tems d'agréer les Affurances de fa haute Confideration.

(Signé)   MALMESBURY.

A Lille, ce 8 Juillet 1797.

(No. 14. B.)   Translation.

The Minister Plenipotentiary of His Britannick Majesty has the Honor of presenting to the Ministers Plenipotentiary of the French Republick, in consequence of the Wish expressed by them in the Conference of this Morning, the following Note: Which he requests them at the same Time to consider, not so much in the Light of an official Paper, as of a verbal and confidential Communication, and as a Proof of his Readiness to facilitate the Progress of the Negotiation, by giving them, on the very Outset, all the Explanations in his Power on the Projet of the Treaty which he has delivered to them.

If, as the Ministers Plenipotentiary of the French Republick have assured him, it is contrary to their most positive Instructions to enter into any Discussion relative to the Cession of those Possessions which belonged to France before the War, it is useless to dwell on the VIth Article: Since the Compensations which his Britannick Majesty might have demanded by that Article, in Return for the Restitutions which He is disposed to make for the Re-establishment of Peace, must, in consequence of this Declaration, be sought for in the Cessions to be made by His Catholick Majesty, and the Batavian Republick.

Lord Malmesbury therefore proposes to insert in the Thirteenth Article, after the Words *Status ante Bellum*, the following Words: " With the Exception of the Island of Trinidad, which shall remain " in full Possession of His Britannick Majesty."

Lord Malmesbury imagines that it is unnecessary for him to repeat the Reasons which induce him to insist upon the retaining of this Conquest, unless compensation should be made for it by some other Cession which shall balance the augmentation of Power accruing to France, from the acquisition of the Spanish part of St. Domingo.

With

With regard to the Fourteenth Article, Lord Malmesbury proposes, that after the Words *Status ante Bellum*, should be added, "With the Exception "of the Town, Fort, and Establishment of the "Cape of Good Hope, and of the Possessions "which belonged to the Dutch before the War in "the Island of Ceylon, and of the Town and Fort "of Cochin, which shall be ceded to His Britan- "nick Majesty in Exchange for the Town of Nega- "patnam and its Dependencies."

Lord Malmesbury repeats to the Ministers Plenipotentiary of the French Republick, the Assurance of his Readiness to concur with them, in every Thing which shall depend on him, to bring the Negotiation to a happy Issue; and requests of them, at the same Time, to accept the Assurances of his high Consideration.

(Signed) MALMESBURY.

Lille, July 8, 1797.

(No. 15. C.) Note from the French Plenipotentiaries to Lord Malmesbury.

Les Ministres Plenipotentiaires de la Republique Françoise ont reçu la Note que le Ministre Plenipotentiaire de Sa Majesté Britannique leur a fait l'Honneur de leur addresser Hier. Ils vont y donner, ainsi qu'au Projet de Traité auquel elle est relative, la plus serieuse Attention. En attendant qu'ils puissent communiquer au Lord Malmesbury les Observations dont ces deux Pieces leur ont parû susceptibles, ils croyent devoir l'inviter à se rendre à la Salle des Conférences demain à Une Heure après midi, si ce Moment lui paroit convenable, pour s'occuper avec lui d'Objets particuliers dont la Discussion peut s'isoler et se suivre sans Rétard.

Ils

Ils prient le Lord Malmesbury d'agréer l'Assurance de leur haute Consideration.

   (Signé(LE TOURNEUR.
        PLEVILLE LE PELLEY,
        HUGUES B, MARET.

Lille, le 21 Messidor,
An 5me de la Republique.

   COLCHEN, Sec. Gen. de la Legation.

(No. 15. C.)   Translation.

THE Ministers Plenipotentiary of the French Republick have received the Note which the Minister Plenipotentiairy of His Britannick Majesty did them the Honor of addressing to them Yesterday. They will give to it, as well as to the project of a Treaty to which it relates, the most serious Attention. In the mean time, though they are not yet enabled to communicate to Lord Malmesbury the Remarks to which these two Papers appear to them liable, they think it their Duty to propose to him a Conference to-morrow, at One o'Clock, if that Hour is agreeable to him, in order to treat with him on <u>distinct Points</u>, the discussion of which may be entered upon <u>separately</u>, and which may be proceded in without Delay.

They request Lord Malmesbury to accept the Assurances of their high Consideration.

   (Signed) LE TOURNEUR.
        PLEVILLE LE PELLEY.
        HUGUES B. MARET.

Lille, 21 Messidor,
5th Year of the Republick.
 (July 9th, 1797.)

   COLCHEN, Sec. Gen. de la Legation.

            (No.

(No. 16. D.)   Note from the French Plenipotentiaries to Lord Malmesbury, dated Lisle.

Les Miniſtres Plénipotentiaires de la République Françaiſe s'empreſſent de ſatisfaire au Deſir que leur a temoigné le Miniſtre Plénipotentiaire de Sa Majeſté Britannique, en lui envoyant une Note ſur les Trois Points qui ont fait l'Objèt de la Conférence de ce Jour.

1. Ils ont l' Ordre poſitif d'exiger la Renonciation au Titre de Roy de France que porte Sa Majeſté Britannique.

Le Lord Malmeſbury eſt prié d'obſerver qu'il ne s'agit pas ſeulement ici d'une Renonciation aux Droits que l'on pourait prétendre devoir reſulter de cette Qualification, mais encore et poſitivement de la Qualification elle même. L'Etabliſſement de la République Françaiſe, et la Reconnoiſſance de cette Forme de Gouvernement par le Roy d'Angleterre, ne lui permettraient pas de conſerver un Titre qui ſuppoſerait en France l'Exiſtence d'un Ordre de Choſes qui n'eſt plus.

2. Les Miniſtres Plénipotentiaires de la République ſont chargés de demander la Reſtitution des Vaiſſeaux pris ou detruits à Toulon.

L'Angleterre à declaré hautement et formellement qu'elle prenait les Vaiſſeaux en Dépot pour le Roy de France. Ce Dépot eſt ſacré. Il appartient inconteſtablement à la République, qui exerce les Droits et la Souveraineté que l'Angleterre attribuoit à Louis XVII. à l'Epoque de la Priſe de Toulon. Sa Majeſté Britannique ne ſaurait donc, en reconnoiſſant la République Françaiſe, méconnaitre ſon Droit à la Reſtitution dont il s'agit, ou refuſer de la faire ou d'en offrir l'Equivalent.

3. Les Miniſtres Plénipotentiaires ont à demander, et demandent la Renonciation de Sa Majeſté Britannique à l' Hypothèque ſur la Belgique.

Ce Pays avait été engagé pour les Emprunts faits par l'Empereur en Angleterre. Il eſt devenu Partie
intégrante

intégrante de la Republique, et ne peut rester grévé d'une semblable Hypothèque.

Les Ministres Plenipotentiaires de la Republique Françaife prient le Lord Malmefbury d'agréer l'Affurance de leur haute Confideration,

   (Signé) LE TOURNEUR.
        PLEVILLE LE PELLEY.
        HUGUES B. MARET.

Lille, 22 Messidor,
l'An 5 de la Republique
      COLCHEN. Sec. Gen. de la Legation.

(No. 16. D.)   Translation.

The Ministers Plenipotentiary of the French Republick lose no Time in complying with the Wish expressed to them by the Minister Plenipotentiary of His Britannick Majesty, by transmitting to him a Note on the Three points which were the Subject of their Conference of this Day.

1. They have positive Orders to require the Renunciation of the Title of King of France borne by His Britannick Majesty.

Lord Malmesbury is requested to observe that the Question is not only of a Renunciation of the Rights which might be pretended to be derived from this Title, but further and formally of the Title itself. The Establishment of the French Republick, and the Acknowledgement of this Form of Government by the King of England, will not allow of his retaining a Title which would imply the Existence in France of an Order of Things which is at an End.

2. The Ministers Plenipotentiary of the Republick are ordered to demand the Restitution of the Vessels taken or destroyed at Toulon.

Great Britain has publicly and formally declared that these Vessels were taken in Trust for the King of France. This Trust is sacred. It incontestably belongs to the Republick, which exercises the Rights and the Sovereignty that Great Britain attributed to
            Louis

Louis XVII. at the period of the Capture of Toulon. His Britannick Majesty cannot, therefore, in acknowledging the French Republick, deny its Right to the Restitution required, or refuse either to make the Restitution, or to offer an Equivalent for it.

ˣ 3. The Ministers Plenipotentiary have Orders to demand, and do demand, the Renunciation, on the part of His Britannick Majesty, of the Mortgage on Belgium.

That Country was mortgaged for the Loans made by the Emperor in England. It has become an integral part of the French Republic, and cannot remain burthened with such a Mortgage.

The Ministers Plenipotentiary of the French Republic request Lord Malmesbury to accept the Assurance of their Consideration.

   (Signed) LE TOURNEUR.
        PLEVILLE LE PELLEY.
        HUGUES B. MARET.

Lille, le 22 Messidor,
5th Year of the Republick,
(July 10, 1797.

    COLCHEN, Sec. Gen. of the Legation

(No. 17.) Extract of a Dispatch from Lord Grenville to Lord Malmesbury, dated Downing-Street, July 13, 1797.

WITH respect to the Demands contained in the Note transmitted to your Lordship by the French Ministers, they have been naturally received here with great Surprize. On the Subject of the Netherlands as connected with the Austrian Loans, it is conceived that any Explanation between His Majesty ˣ and the French Government is wholly unnecessary. The Loans raised in England for the Service of the Emperor of Germany, and guaranteed by Act of Parliament here, rest, as your Lordship will perceive, by the annexed Copy of the Convention on that Subject; upon the Security of all the Revenues
               of

of all the hereditary Dominions of His Imperial Majesty. They do not seem in any Manner to come under the Description contained in the Sixth Article of the Preliminaries between Austria and France, respecting Mortgages upon the Soil of the Netherlands, on which Ground alone France could have any Pretence to interfere in the Business. Nor is this Subject One which appears to be in any Manner a fit Point of Discussion between His Majesty and the Republick; the King neither forms nor has any Intention of forming any Demand on the French Government for the Payment of any Part either of the Interest or Capital of those Loans. It is to the Emperor alone that His Majesty looks for the Performance of his Imperial Majesty's Engagements to Him, and it is upon the Austrian Government, and upon its Revenues, that Individuals concerned in those Loans have Claims of private Right, and Means of Personal Demand secured to them by the Convention.

On the other Two Points I have nothing to add to the Observations which your Lordship has already made upon them: And we can therefore only wait with Impatience for the Answer to the Projet delivered by your Lordship, which will enable us to form a Judgment on the Intentions of the Government with whom we are treating.

Right Honourable Lord Malmesbury.

(No. 18.)   Extract of a Dispatch from Lord Malmesbury to Lord Grenville, dated Lisle, 16th July 1797.

IT was at the express Invitation of the French Plenipotentiaries that I met them on Thursday the 13th instant; *One of them* stated their Motive for wishing to confer with me, not to be in consequence of any Answer they had received from Paris on the Subject of the *Projet*, which he observed could not be expected so soon, but to resume the Discussion on the Article which he had objected to on my first reading the *Projet*, and on which they conceived it

was

was possible and even expedient to argue before we entered on the more important Branches of the Negotiation. It was Article II. that he referred to. He objected to the Renewal of the Treaties therein mentioned from various Reasons; First, That many and even most of them were irrelevant to that we were now negotiating; Secondly, That they were in Contradiction to the new Order of Things established in France, as they seem to imply an Acknowledgement that a Portion of the Regal Authority is still existing; Thirdly, That they might be supposed to apply to Conventions and Stipulations, in direct Contradiction to their present Form of Government, and he quoted the Convention of Pilnitz in particular. I was about to reply to him, and I trust in a Way that would have done away his Apprehensions on this point, when *another of them* interposed by saying, That their sincere and only desire was that the Treaty we were now entering upon might be so framed, as to secure permanently the Object for which it was intended; that no Article likely to produce this end might be omitted, nor any doubtful one inserted; but that the whole, as well with regard to the past as to the future, might be so clearly and distinctly expressed, that no room for Cavil might be left. This he assured me, in the Name of his Colleagues, was all that was meant by their Objection to renew so many Treaties in which such various Interests were blended, and so many Points discussed foreign to the present Moment. Their renewing them in a Lump, and without examining carefully to what we were pledged by them, might involve us in difficulties much better to be avoided. I replied, that I admitted most certainly all he said, and that it was with this View and on this principle solely that the Renewal of these Treaties was proposed by His Majesty; and that if he recollected (as he undoubtedly did) the different Wars which were terminated by these Treaties, and the many important Regulations

tions stipulated by them, he would admit that the allowing them to remain in their full Force was simply an Acknowledgement of the Tenure by which almost all the Sovereigns of Europe, and particularly the French Republick, held their Dominions up to this Day. That these Treaties were become the Law of Nations, and that infinite Confusion would result from their not being renewed.

He replied, that our Object was evidently the same, that we only differed as to the Manner. I thought the renewing these Treaties *in toto* would the best contribute to it; while they were inclined to think, that extracting from them every Thing which immediately related to the Interests of the Two Countries and stating it in One Article, was more likely to attain this desirable Object. *The French Minister* again repeated, that their First Wish was, that the Treaty we were now making should be clear, distinct, solid, and lasting and such a one, as could not, at any future period, be broken through without a manifest Violation of good Faith. And I again repeated, that nothing could be so consonant to my Orders, or the Intentions of my Royal Master.

One of the French Plenipotentiaries was disposed to dwell on his Objections, which were, that these Treaties were signed when France was a Monarchy, and that any Retrospect to those Times implied a Sort of Censure on their present Form of Government; but this was arguing on such weak Ground, and so incapable of being seriously maintained, that I, to avoid superfluous Contradiction, was very willing to let it pass unnoticed. After a good deal of very conciliatory, and even amicable discussion, which, however, neither Party gave much Way to the other, it was proposed by them that we should return Home, to meet again as soon as was convenient after an attentive and deliberate perusal of the Treaties, in order to state respectively our Ideas on this Subject. I observed, that although I was perfectly prepared to do it it at the Moment, and felt almost bold enough to affirm, that no Measure could be devised which would so completely meet our Intentions as an unreserved Renewal of the Treaties they hesitated about, yet I was very willing to acquiesce in their Proposal, with this simple Observation, that if any Delay arose from it, such Delay was imputable to them and not to me. My words were, "Je ne me rends pas responsable "des Longueurs dans lesquelles cette Discussion "pourrait nous entrainer." The French Minister's Answer was, "Si des Longueurs servent à déter- "miner des Objets qui pourraient donner lieu à des "Querelles à l'avenir, ce sera du Tems bien em- "ployé." It was not my Wish to contest this Assertion, and our Conference ended with it.

(No. 19.)　　Extracts of a Dispatch from Lord Malmsbury to Lord Grenville, dated Lisle, July 16, 1797.

My Lord,

YESTERDAY at the Moment I was preparing to attend the Conference, in which we were to enter into fuller Discussions on the litigated Subject of the Renewal of the Treaties mentioned in the Second Article of the Projet, I received from the French Legation the inclosed paper (A). In about an Hour I returned the enclosed Answer (B), to which I received the enclosed Reply (C); and I am this Moment come from the Conference which has taken place in consequence of it.

I began by saying, that I had solicited this Interview from the same Motive which would actuate every part of my Conduct; that I wished to make my Reports not only correct but conciliatory as far as depended on me, and I now was come in order, if possible, to obtain from them such Comments and Explanations of the Note they sent to me Yesterday, as would enable me, when I transmitted it to my Court, to secure the Negotiation from being interrupted, perhaps abruptly terminated, by the perusal

of

of it. If I underſtood it right, it meant that the Directory requires as *a sine qua non Preliminary*, that every thing the King has conquered from all and each of His Enemies ſhould be reſtored, and that till this Reſtoration was conſented to the Negotiation was not even to begin. I ſaid, if I was correct in this Statement, and the plain Senſe of the Declaration would bear no other Interpretation, I muſt add that it would not only moſt certainly prevent the Treaty from beginning, but would leave no Room for treating at all, ſince it deprived His Majeſty of every Means of Negotiation; for I could not ſuppoſe that it was in their Thoughts to intimate that the Principle of Treaty, as far as it related to His Majeſty, was to be One of all Ceſſion and no Compenſation, and yet that was preciſely the poſition in which His Majeſty was placed by their Note.

One of the French Plenipotentiaries, who had let me proceed rather reluctantly, here ſtopt me, and ſaid, that he and his Colleagues were exceedingly happy that I had expreſſed a Wiſh to ſee them before I diſpatched my Meſſenger; that they wiſhed to aſſure me, that they had thought it dealing fairly and honorably to ſtate what they had received from the Directory in the very Words in which it came to them; that they ſhould be ſorry if the Declaration they had been directed to make me, ſhould be of a Nature to interrupt, much leſs to break off, the Negotiation; that it was the ſincere Wiſh of the Directory that the Negotiation ſhould proceed and end ſucceſsfully; and that, far from ſhutting the door to further Diſcuſſions, they were perfectly ready to hear any propoſals we had to make, and only wiſhed that theſe propoſals ſhould be, if poſſible, ſuch as were compatible with their moſt ſacred Engagements. I repeated what I had ſaid, that no door was left open if His Majeſty was *in limine* to reſtore every Thing; and that a Peace on theſe Conditions would not be heard of by the Country. I

obſerved,

observed, that immediately on leaving them, I should dispatch a Messenger; but what that Messenger carried would most materially affect the progress and Issue of the Negotiation; I therefore desired to know whether, in consequence of what I had heard from them, <u>I might consider the strict and literal Meaning of the Declaration not to be a decided Negative</u> (which it certainly seemed to imply) <u>on all compensation whatever to be made to His Majesty, but that proposals tending to this Effect would be listened to.</u> *One of them* answered, " certainly, and " if they should be found such as it will be impossible " for us to admit, we will on our Side bring forward " others for your Court to deliberate on." Under this Assurance, which at least, <u>to a certain Degree, qualifies the Declaration of Yesterday,</u> I broke up the Conference.

(No. 20. A.)   Note from the French Plenipotentiaries to Lord Malmesbury.

Les Ministres Plenipotentiaires de la Republique Française ont fait passer à leur Gouvernement le Projet de Traité et la Note relative, qui leur ont été presentés le 20 du present Mois, par le Ministre Plénipotentiaire de Sa Majesté Britannique.

Ils viennent de recevoir des Communications nouvelles et des Ordres en conséquence desquels ils doivent faire au Lord Malmesbury la Declaration suivante.

Il existe dans les Traités patents et secrets qui lient la République Française à ses Alliés, l'Espagne et la Republique Batave, des Articles portant garantie respective des Territoires que les Trois Puissances possedaient avant la Guerre. Le Gouvernement Français, ne pouvant pas se délier des Engagemens qu'il a contractés par ces Traités, établit comme Preliminaire indispensable de la Négotiation pour la Paix avec l'Angleterre, le Consentement de Sa Majesté Britannique à la Restitution de toutes les Possessions

qu'elle

qu'elle occupe, non feulement fur la République Française, mais encore et formellement fur l'Efpagne et la République Batave.

En conféquence, les Miniftres Plénipotentiaires fouffignés invitent Lord Malmefbury à s'expliquer fur cette Reftitution, et à y confentir s'il y eft fuffifamment autorifé ; fi non, et dans le Cas contraire à envoyer un Courier à fa Cour pour en obtenir les Pouvoirs néceffaires.

L'Objet de la Conférence qui devoit avoir lieu ce Jour, fe trouvant néceffairement ajourné par l'Effet de la Déclaration ci-deffus, Les Miniftres Plénipotentiaires de la République ont à témoigner au Lord Malmefbury le Regret qu'ils eprouvent de manquer cette Occafion qu'ils avaient recherchée de s'entretenir avec lui : Au furplus, dans le Cas où le Lord Malmefbury auroit quelque Communication à leur faire, ils le prient de croire qu'ils fe font toujours empreffés de le recevoir et de l'entendre quand il le jugera à propos.

Ils le prient en même Tems d'agréer de nouveau l'Affurance de leur haute Confideration.

(Signé)   LE TOTRNEUR.
PLEVILLE LE PELLEY.
HUGUES B. MARET.

Lille, 27 Meffidor,
l'An 5 de la Republique.

COLCHEN, Sec. Gen. de la Legation.

(No, 20. A.)   Tranflation.

THE Minifters Plenipotentiary of the French Republick have tranfmitted to their Government the Project of the Treaty, and the Note relating thereto, which were delivered to them the 20th of the prefent Month, by the Minifter Plenipotentiary of His Britannick Majefty.

They

They have just received fresh Communications and Orders, which require that they should make the following Declaration to Lord Malmesbury.

There exist in the Public and Secret Treaties, by which the French Republic is bound to its Allies, Spain and the Batavian Republick, Articles by which the Three Powers respectively guarantee the Territories possessed by each of them before the War.

The French Government, unable to detach itself from the Engagements which it has contracted by these Treaties, establishes, as an indispensable Preliminary of the Negotiation for the Peace with England, the Consent of His Britannick Majesty to the Restitution of all the Possessions which He occupies, not only from the French Republick, but further and formally of those of Spain and the Batavian Republick.

In consequence, the Undersigned Ministers Plenipotentiary request Lord Malmesbury to explain himself with regard to this Restitution, and to consent to it, if he is sufficiently authorized to do so; if not, and in the contrary Case, to send a Messenger to his Court, in order to procure the necessary Powers.

The Object of the Conference which was to have taken place to Day being necessarily delayed by the Purport of the abovementioned Declaration, the Ministers Plenipotentiary of the Republick have to express to Lord Malmesbury the Regret that they feel in losing this Opportunity of conversing together, which they had themselves solicited:—But in case Lord Malmesbury should have any Communication to make to them, they beg him to believe that they will always be happy to receive him, and to listen to him, whenever he may think it proper.

They requeſt him, at the ſame Time, to accept anew the Aſſurances of their high Conſideration.

(Signed) LE TOURNEUR.
PLEVILLE LE PELLEY.
HUGHES B. MARET.

Liſle, 27th Meſſidor,
5 Year of the Republick.
(July 15, 1797.)

COLCHEN, Sec. Gen. of the Legation.

(No. 21. B.) Note from Lord Malmeſbury to the French Plenipotentiaries.

Le Miniſtre Plénipotentiaire de Sa Majeſté Britannique a prêté l'Attention la plus ſerieuſe à la Note, en Date de ce Matin, qu'il vient de recevoir de la Part des Miniſtres Plénipotentiaires de la République Françaiſe.

Il n'héſite pas à leur déclarer que ſes Inſtructions ne l'autoriſent nullement à admettre, comme Principe Préliminaire, celui que leur Daclaration parait vouloir etablir: Cependant, etant perſuadé que ſon premier Devoir eſt, de ne renoncer à l'Eſpoir d'une Conciliation que lorſqu'il aura épuiſé tous les Moyens d'y arriver, et voulant écarter, dans le Rapport qu'il aura à faire à ſa Cour, ſur un Objet auſſi important, la Poſſibilité de toute Méſintelligence, il leur demandera pour Demain, et à l'Heure qui pourra leur convenir, une Conférence, à la ſuite de laquelle il ſe propoſe d'expédier un Courier à ſa Cour.

Il prie les Miniſtres Plénipotentiaires de la Republique Françaiſe d'agréer les Aſſurances de ſa haute Conſideration.

(Singé) MALMESBURY.

A Lille, ce 15 Juillet 1797.

(Note 21. B.) Tranſlation.

The Miniſter Plenipotentiary of His Britannick Majeſty has given the moſt ſerious Attention to the Note dated this Morning, which he has received

I from

from the Ministers Plenipotentiary of the French Republick.

He has no Hesitation in declaring to them, that his Instructions by no Means authorize him to admit, as a preliminary Principle, that which their Declaration seems intended to establish: Nevertheless, being persuaded that it is his first Duty not to give up the Hopes of Conciliation until he shall shall have exhausted every Means of obtaining it, and being anxious to avoid, in the Report which he shall have to make to his Court, the possibility of Misunderstanding on a Subject of such Importance, he proposes to them a Conference for To-morrow, at the Hour most convenient to them, after which it is his Intention to dispatch a Messenger to his Court.

He requests the Ministers Plenipotentiary of the French Republic to accept the Assurance of his high Consideration.

     (Signed) MALMESBURY.

Lisle, 15th July, 1797.

(No. 22. C.) Note from the French Plenipotentiaries to Lord Malmesbury.

Les Ministres Plénipotentiaires de la République Françoise, s'empressent d'accéder au Desir que leur témoigne le Ministre Plenipotentiaire de Sa Majesté Britannique, de conférer avec eux sur l'Objèt de la Note qu'ils lui ont adressée ce Jour.

Ils ont en conséquence l'Honneur de lui proposer de se rendre Demain, à onze Heures du Matin, au Lieu ordinaire des Conferences.

Ils le prient d'agréer l'Assurance de leur haute consideration.

  (Signé) LE TOURNEUR.
       PLEVILLE LE PELLEY.
       HUGUES B. MARET.

Lille, le 27 Messidor,
An 5 de la République,
une et indivisible.

    COLCHEN, Sec. Gen. de la Legation.

(No.

(No. 22. C.)   Translation.

The Ministers Plenipotentiary of the French Republick lose no Time in acceding to the Desire expressed by the Minister Plenipotentiary of His Britannick Majesty, of conferring with them on the Subject of the Note which they addressed to him this Day.

They have in consequence the Honour of proposing to him to meet To-morrow Morning at Eleven o'Clock, at the usual place of Conference.

They request him to accept the Assurances of their high Consideration.

   (Signed) LE TOURNEUR.
         PLEVILLE LE PELLEY.
         HUGUES B. MARET.

Lisle, the 27th Messidor,
5th Year of the Republick,
 one and indivisible.
(July 15, 1797.)
    COLCHEN. Sec. Gen. of the Legation.

(No. 23.) Copy of a Dispatch from Lord Grenville to Lord Malmesbury, dated Downing Street, July 20, 1797.

My Lord,

Your Lordship's Dispatches by the Messenger Dressins, were received here on the 17th Instant, at Night, and I lost no Time in receiving His Majesty's Commands on the very important Subject of your Letter, No. 9.

I am much concerned to be under the Necessity of remarking, that the Claim brought forward in the Note transmitted to your Lordship by the French Plenipotentiaries, is in itself so extravagant, and so little to be reconciled either with the former Professions of those Ministers, or with their Conduct in the previous Stages of the Negociation, that it affords the strongest Presumption of a Determination o preclude all Means of Accommodation. If such is really the Determination of the Directory, nothing can remain for this Country but to perſevere in oppoſing, with an Energy and Spirit proportioned to the Exigency, a Syſtem which muſt tend to perpetuate a State of War and Civil Tumult in every Part of Europe.

The natural Step upon the preſent Occaſion would therefore have been to direct your Lordſhip to terminate at once a Negotiation, which, on the Footing now propoſed by the Enemy, affords neither the Hope nor the Means of any favourable Concluſion. Nothing being left for Treaty, where, as a Preliminary Step, one Party is required to concede every Thing, and all compenſation from the other is abſolutely and at once precluded. His Majeſty's Servants have, however, obſerved, that in the Concluſion of your Lordſhip's Conference with the French Plenipotentiaries on the Subject of the Note in Queſtion, the Preſident of that Miſſion informed your Lordſhip, that it was not intended to reſiſt all Compenſation for the immenſe Extent of Reſtitution demanded from His Majeſty, and for the other obvious circumſtances of diſadvantage to this Country in the Situation of Europe, as reſulting from the War; and even added, that he and his Colleagues would eventually bring forward Propoſals on this Head for the Deliberation of the King's Government. It appeared poſſible that ſome Advantage might perhaps ariſe to the great Object of Peace, from grounding on this Declaration a further Proceeding, ſuch as might afford to the Directory (if they are ſo diſpoſed) the Means of replacing the Negotiation on a more practicable Footing. With the View therefore of leaving nothing untried which can contribute to reſtore Peace on any ſuitable Terms, His Majeſty has been pleaſed to direct that your Lordſhip ſhould for that Purpoſe aſk another Conference with the French Plenipotentiaries. In this Conference your Lordſhip will remark in ſuch Terms as the Occaſion muſt naturally ſuggeſt to you upon the indefenſible Spirit and Tendency of the

Demand

Demand now made by France. You will observe that France, treating in Conjunction with her Allies, and, in their Name, cannot with any Pretence of Justice and Fairness, oppose her treaties with them as an Obstacle in the Way of any reasonable Proposal of Peace in which they are to be included. In a separate Negotiation, to which they were not parties, such a plea might, perhaps, have been urged; but in that case France would have been bound to offer, from her own Means, that Compensation which she did not think herself at Liberty to engage to obtain from her Allies. And such was, in Fact, as your Lordship must remember, the Principle on which His Majesty offered to treat last Year, when he was really bound, by Engagements to Austria, similar to those which are now alledged by France. But it never can be allowed that France, Spain, and Holland, negotiating jointly for a Peace with Great Britain, can set up, as a Bar to our just Demands, the Treaties between themselves, from which they are at onceable to release each other whenever they think fit.

You will further remark, that even if, contrary to all Reason, such a Principle could for a Moment have been admitted on our Part, still even that Principle, inadmissible as it is, could only apply to public Treaties, known to those who agreed to be governed by them, and not to secret Articles, unknown even to the French Plenipotentiaries, or concealed by One of them from the Knowledge of the others.

You will add in explicit, though not offensive Terms, that the Whole of this Pretence now set up by France is incontestably frivolous and illusory; being grounded on a Supposition of a State of Things directly contrary to that which is known really to exist. It being perfectly notorious that both Spain and Holland, so far from wishing to continue the War, were compelled by France to engage in it, greatly against their own Wishes; and to undertake,

with-

without the Means of supporting it, a Contest in which they had nothing to gain, and every Thing to lose. It never therefore can be allowed to be a Question of any possible Doubt, but that the Directory, if they really wish it, must already have obtained, or could at any Moment obtain, the Consent of those Powers to such Terms of Peace as have been proposed by His Majesty. If, however, France, from any Motive of Interest or Engagement, is in Truth desirous to procure for them the Restitution of Possessions which they were unable to defend, and have no Means to reconquer, the Project delivered by your Lordship afforded an Opening for this: those Articles having been so drawn as to leave it to France to provide a Compensation to His Majesty, either out of her own Colonies, or out of those of her Allies, respectively conquered by His Majesty's Arms. The Choice between these Alternatives may be left to the Directory; but to refuse both is, in other Words, <u>to refuse all Compensation</u>. This is nevertheless <u>expresly declared not to be the Intention of those with whom you treat</u>. It is therefore necessary that your Lordship should demand from them a Statement of the Proposals, which, as they informed you, they have to make, in order to do away this apparent <u>Contradiction</u>, which the King's Servants are wholly unable to reconcile by any Suggestion of theirs, even if it were fitting and reasonable for them to bring forward any <u>new Proposals</u> immediately after the detailed <u>Project</u> which was delivered on the Part of this Country at the Outset of the Negotiation.

Since that Project is not acceded to, we have evidently, and on every Ground, a Right to expect a <u>Counter Project</u>, equally full and explicit on the Part of the Enemy. You will therefore state to the French Ministers distinctly, that the only Hope of bringing this Business to a favourable Conclusion, is by their stating at once plainly, and without Reserve, the Whole of what they have to ask, instead of bring-

ing

ing forward separate Points one after the other, not only contrary to the avowed Principle of the Negotiation proposed by themselves, but, as it appears, even contrary to the Expectation of the Ministers themselves who are employed on the Part of France. There can be no Pretence for refusing a Compliance with this Demand, if the Plenipotentiaries of France are disposed to forward the Object of Peace: And the obtaining such a Statement from them is, as I have before stated to your Lordship, a Point of so much Importance, in any Course which this Negotiation may take, that it is the King's Pleasure that your Lordship should use every possible Endeavour to prevent their eluding so just a Demand.

After what has passed, it is, I fear, very doubtful whether such a Counter Project would be framed on Principles such as could be admitted here; but it would at all Events place the Business on its real Issue, and bring distinctly into Question the several Points on which the Conclusion of Peace, or the Prolongation of War, will really depend.

        I am, &c.
    (Signed) GRENVILLE.

Right Honourable Lord Malmesbury.

(No. 24.) Copy of a Dispatch from Lord Grenville to Lord Malmesbury, dated Downing-Street, July 20, 1797.

My Lord,

THERE are Two separate Points on which it is necessary for me to say a few Words to your Lordship, in Addition to the Instructions in my other Dispatch, on the General Subject of the Negociation.

The First relates to the Assertion of One of the French Ministers, "that the Portuguese Ships and Troops were at Toulon." The Fact is very immaterial as to any Conclusion that could be drawn from it, to affect the Situation or just Claims of the Court of of Lisbon; because your Lordship well knows, that it is a Principle universally recognized in the public Law of Europe, that when One of the Parties, in a Defensive Alliance, furnishes to his Ally the stipulated Succours, those Succours remain entirely at the Disposal of the requiring Party, to be employed wherever he shall judge proper, subject only to the Limitations of the Treaty which before existed; and if the Amount of those Succours is not encreased beyond that engaged for, nor the Means of using them extended by new Facilities, the Party furnishing the stipulated Assistance is not understood to violate the Laws of Neutrality.

But the Fact, in this Case, would not bear out the Assertion, even if the Argument to be drawn from it were more conclusive. The Troops of Her Most Faithful Majesty having been, as I apprehend, no otherwise employed than in the Two Campaigns carried on by Land, upon the Southern Part of the Frontiers of France and Spain.

The other point relates to what was said to your Lordship about the Treaty of Pilnitz. It would certainly not require much Argument to prove that the Renewal of several Treaties enumerated by Name and Date, and the latest of which was concluded in 1783, does not imply a Renewal of another Treaty supposed to be concluded in 1791. But what is more material to the present Case is, that your Lordship should take this Oppertunity to explain, in the most distinct and unequivocal Terms, that if any secret Treaty was in fact concluded at the Interview at Pilnitz, between the late Emperor, and the King of Prussia (which is, to say the least, very doubtful in point of Fact), this at least is certain, that His Majesty was no Party to such Treaty; and not only was not then included in it, but has never since adhered to it, nor even been apprized of its Contents. The publick Declaration which was made at that Interview, shews on the Face of it that

His

His Majesty was no party to it; and it is, indeed, notorious that it applied to Circumstances which were done away long before the War broke out between Austria and France, and that the subsequent Negotiations for the Maintenance of Peace between those Powers turned on points wholly distinct from those supposed to have been referred to in the pretended Treaty of Pilnitz.

This Explanation, however little connected with the present Negotiation, seems to be called for by the Allusion made to you upon the Subject; and, indeed, on a point on which so much Misrepresentation has prevailed, it is useful not to omit the Opportunity of stating the Facts as they really are.

I am, &c.
(Signed) GRENVILLE.

Right Honourable Lord Malmesbury.

(No. 25.)   Extract of a Dispatch from Lord Malmesbury to Lord Grenville, dated Lisle, 25th, July 1797.

My Lord,

I HAVE the Honour to acknowledge your Lordship's Dispatches, No. 19 and 20, of the 20th inst. which were delivered to me on Saturday the 22d inst. by the Messenger Major.

It was impossible that the Claim brought forward in the Note inclosed in my No. 9, could have produced on your Lordship's Mind any Impression different from that which you describe, and I am happy to find that the Conduct I observed, when it was first delivered to me, was such as put it in my power to execute with great Consistency the spirited Instructions your Lordship now sends me.

Immediately on the Arrival of the Messenger, I proposed an Interview with the French Plenipotentiaries, and we met on Sunday the 23d, at One P. M.

K   I could

I could not obey His Majesty's Orders in a Manner more likely to command Attention, and to impress those who heard me with a just Sense of the Mixture of Firmness and Moderation with which His Majesty was pleased to conduct this important Negociation, than by employing not only the Substance, but as far as was practicable in Conversation, <u>the very Words</u> of your Lordship's Dispatch, No. 19; and if I should attempt to relate minutely what I myself said in this Conference, it would in Fact be little more than a Repetition of them.

I began by observing, that I was certain the French Plenipotentiaries must be fully prepared for what I now had it in Command to say: I reminded them that I had taken upon me to affirm when we were last assembled, and immediately before I dispatched my Messenger, that the requiring <u>such a Preliminary</u> as that proposed in the Note, was <u>putting an End at once to all Negotiation</u>, and that I was sure Peace <u>on such Terms would not</u> be <u>heard</u> of; that the Orders I was then about to communicate to them would prove that I had not made this Assertion lightly, or in consequence of any hasty Opinion of my own, at the same Time that it would also appear that my Royal Master was as anxiously and as sincerely inclined to listen to all reasouable and admissible Conditions, as He was determined to repel and reject all such as were of an opposite Description. I then, my Lord, took up my Arguments on the precise Grounds set forth in your Lordship's, No. 19. I neither omitted any Thing, nor inserted any Thing of my own, which could at all alter its Spirit; and I only varied from the Letter inasmuch as was necessary to make it applicable to a Conference

My First Object was to state, in as forcible a way as possible, the utter Inadmissibility of the Pretension set forth in the Note, the frivolous and illusory Reasons alledged for bringing it forward, and I observed that, if it was persevered in, it must be lead to this

necessary

necessary Conclusion, that there did exist when it was framed an Intention on the part of the Directory to break off the Negotiation in the Outset. My Second Object in point of Reasoning, though a very primary One in point of Importance, was either to prevent the Negotiation breaking off at all, or if this was not to be prevented, to endeavour to be so clear and explicit in my Language, and to draw the Line so distinctly between such Sacrifices as His Majesty might be inclined to make in order to restore so great a Blessing as Peace, and those to which the Dignity of His Crown and Interest of His Subjects would never allow him to attend, as to make it impossible that by any future Cavil or Subterfuge the Interruption of the Treaty, if unfortunately it should be interrupted, could be imputed to any other Cause than the exorbitant demands of the French Government; and the better to insure this purpose, I explained to them that His Majesty having already in a detailed Projet stated freely and fully His Conditions, and these Conditions having been at once rejected by a sweeping Claim on the Part of the French Government, it was not fitting or reasonable, neither could it be expected that any new Proposals should originate with His Majesty: And that on every Ground the King had a Right to expect a *Contre-Projet* from them, stating at once plainly and without Reserve the Whole of what they had to ask, instead of bringing forward separate points, One after another, directly contrary to the principle on which we had agreed to begin the Negotiation, and which, from their being insulated, could only tend to protract and impede its progress.

On the First Point, on the Inadmissibility of the preliminary Conditions as proposed by the French Government, *One of the French Plenipotentiaries* said, it was impossible for them to do more than to take it for Reference, that the Instructions they had received when the Directory sent them the Note, were precise and

and positive, and that they had received none since. He therefore had on that Point simply to request of me, that I would state in Writing the several Grounds on which His Majesty rejected this Proposition, in order that the Report transmitted by them to the Directory might be correct; and he assured me, that if I did not think it proper to put in Writing all the Arguments I had used to them in the Conference, they would have no Scruple of employing those I omitted in such a Way as was the best calculated to give them Weight, and to use *the French Minister's* own Expression, to place the Negociation once more on its Legs.

In regard to the Second Point, he had no hesitation in agreeing with me, that the best Method, and indeed the only One, which could accelerate the Whole of the Business, was for them to give in a *Contre-Projet*, neither did he attempt to disprove our perfect Right to expect One from them before we made any new Proposals. But he said, that it was not necessary for him to observe that as long as they were bound by their Instructions not to give way on the Proposition, I had now so decidedly rejected, that it was impossible for them to move a Step without new Orders from the Directory; that they would ask for these Orders immediately, and lose no time in acquainting me when they were received.

I observed, that in our last Conference he had intimated to me they were empowered to come to some Explanation with me on the Subject of Compensation to be made to His Majesty for the great Cessions he was disposed to make; that, at the time, I conceived these Explanations were of a Nature to qualify the wide claim stated in the Note, and that if I had abstained from pressing him further at the moment, it was from perceiving a Reluctance on their Part to bring them forward:—That, however, if they really had such Proposals to make me, and if they were of a Nature to meet in Substance and Effect sect the Basis laid down in the Projet I had given, I should be well disposed to listen to them.

One of the French Ministers, after some Hesitation and a Sort of silent Reference to One of his Colleagues, said he thought as Matters now stood, it would be much better to wait their Answer from Paris:—That it was a very important period, a Crisis in the Negotiation, the Result of which probably would be conclusive as to its Fate, and that it seemed to be of more Consequence to make this Result as conformable to what he hoped I was convinced were as much their Wishes as mine, than to waste our Time in Discussions which were useless, not to say more, till this was ascertained.

I confined myself in my Reply to saying, I had no Objection whatever to giving to the French Plenipotentiaries a paper, stating the strong Motives on which His Majesty rejected the proposition made in their Note of the 15th; and that as I, on my part, had considered it a Duty to make my Reports as conciliatory as was consistent with Truth and Correctness, so I heard with great pleasure the Assurances he gave me of their intending to observe the same Line of Conduct.

That as we seemed perfectly agreed as to the propriety of their producing a *Contre-Projet*, I had nothing to say on that point, except to express my most sincere Wish that it would soon appear, and when it did appear, be such a one as would lead to a speedy and satisfactory Conclusion of the Negotiation.

Right Honourable Lord Grenville.

(No. 26.)   Note from Lord Malmesbury to the French Plenipotentiaries.

Le Ministre Plénipotentiaire de Sa Majesté Britannique a fait passer à Sa Cour la Note qui lui a été remise le 15 de ce Mois par les Ministres Plénipotentiaires de la République Française, et ayant reçu les
                                                     Ordres

Ordres du Roi son Maitre à ce Sujet, il s'empresse de leur ré-iterer par ecrit, conformément au Desir qu'ils lui en ont temoigné, les Réflexions suivantes, qu'il leur a deja exposées de vive Voix d'après ses Instructions les plus positives.

Il observe d'abord, que demander, " comme Pré-
" liminaire indispensable de la Négotiation pour la
" Paix avec l'Angleterre, le Consentement de Sa
" Majesté Britannique à la Restitution de toutes les
" Possessions qu'elle occupe, non seulement sur la
" Republique Française, mais encore et formelle-
" ment sur l'Espagne et la Republique Batave,"
c'est vouloir établir une Condition préalable qui ex-
clut toute Réciprocité ; refuse au Roi toute Compensation ; et ne laisse aucun Objet de Négociation ultérieure.

Que la République Française, autorisée par ses Alliés à negocier en leur Nom et formellement les Articles de la Paix, ne sauroit opposer ses Traités partiels avec Eux à des Propositions raisonnables ; puisqu'il est reconnu, que les Parties contractantes conservent toujours le Pouvoir de modifier, d'un consentement mutuel, les conditions auxquelles Elles se feront respectivement engagées, toutes les fois que leurs Intérêts communs pourront l'exiger ;—par con-séquent, la Proposition faite au Roi d'une Restitution générale et gratuite, comme Preliminaire indispensa-ble, supposerait nécessairement à Sa Majesté Catholi-que et à la République Batave, des Dispositions bien moins pacifiques que celles qui animent la Républi-que Française.

Que d'ailleurs, d'après ce qui s'est passé dans les premieres Conférences, le Lord Malmesbury a tou-jours cru devoir s'attendre à ce que le Roi son Maitre fut compensé des Sacrifices qu'il était porté à faire pour la Paix, par la Conservation d'une Partie de Ses Conquêtes ; et il pouvoit d'autant moins pré-voir quelque Obstacle à l'Occasion des Articles Sé-crets des Traités qui lient la Republique Française,

que

que le Principe de Compenfation fut reconnu par une Déclaration formelle et pofitive faite au Nom du Directoire Exécutif, et communiquée dans une Note Officielle en Date du 27 Novembre 1796, Déclaration poftérieure à la Confection de ces Traités.

C'était donc à fin d'applanir autant que poffible toutes les Difficultés, que dans le Projet du Traité que le Lord Malmefbury à remis aux Miniftres Plénipotentiaires de la République Françaife, on laiffa à la France l'Alternative d'établir cette Compenfation fur fes propres Poffeffions, ou fur celles de fes Alliès. —Or, le Refus abfolu de cette Alternative, parait ecarter le feul Moyen poffible de concilier tous les Intérêts, et d'arriver à une Paix jufte, honorable, et permanente.

Le Lord Malmefbury, perfuadé que telle ne fauroit être l'Intention du Gouvernement Français, efpère d'après les Raifons qu'il vient de leur expofer, qu'on ne continuera pas à infifter fur une Condition à la quelle Sa Majefté Britannique ne pourra aucunement Se prêter.

Il prie de nouveau les Miniftres Plenipotentiaires de la Republique Françaife d'agréer les Affurances de fa haute Confideration.

    (Signé) MALMESBURY.

A Lifle, ce 24me Juillet 1797.

(No. 26.)   Tranflation.

The Minifter Plenipotentiary of His Britannick Majefty has tranfmitted to his Court the Note which was delivered to him the 15th of this Month, by the Minifters Plenipotentiary of the French Republick; and having received the Orders of the King his Mafter, on this Subject, he haftens to repeat to them, in Writing, conformably to the Defire which they have expreffed to him, the following Reflections, which he had already ftated to them verbally, in confequence of his moft pofitive Inftructions.

He

He observes, in the first Place, that to require "As an indispensable Preliminary of Negociation for Peace with England, the Consent of His Britannick Majesty to the formal Restitution of all the Possessions which he occupies, as well those of the French Republick, as further and formally those of Spain and the Batavian Republick," is to wish to establish a previous Condition, which excludes all Reciprocity, refuses to the King all Compensation, and leaves no Object of ulterior Negociation.

That the French Republic, formally authorized by its Allies to negociate the Articles of Peace in their Name, cannot fairly set up its partial Treaties with them, in Opposition to reasonable Proposals of Peace, since it is universally understood that the Contracting Parties always preserve the Power to modify, by mutual Consent, the Conditions by which they may be engaged to each other, whenever their common Interests may require it :—Consequently, the Proposition made to the King of a general and gratuitous Restitution as an indispensable Preliminary, would necessarily impute to his Catholick Majesty, and to the Batavian Republick, Dispositions far less pacifick than those which animate the French Republick.

That moreover in consequence of what passed in the first Conferences, Lord Malmesbury has always thought himself entitled to expect that the King His Master would find a Compensation for the Sacrifices He was ready to make for Peace, by retaining a Part of His Conquests; and He was the less able to forsee any Obstacle, on account of the Secret Articles of the Treaties which bind the French Republick, as the Principle of Compensation was acknowledged by a formal and positive Declaration, made in the Name of the Executive Directory, and communicated in an Official Note, dated the 27th of November,

ber 1796; a Declaration, posterior to the Completion of those Treaties.

It was, therefore, in order to remove, as much as possible, every Difficulty that, in the Project of a Treaty, which Lord Malmesbury has delivered to the Ministers Plenipotentiary of the French Republick, the Alternative was left to France to settle this Compensation on its own Possessions, or on those of its Allies: But the absolute Refusal of this Alternative appears to do away the only possible Means of conciliating every Interest, and of arriving at an honourable, just, and permanent Peace.

Lord Malmesbury, persuaded that such cannot be the Intention of the French Government, hopes, that in consequence of the Reasons herein stated, a Condition will not be insisted upon, to which His Britannick Majesty can by no Means consent.

He again requests the Ministers Plenipotentiary of the French Republick to accept the Assurances of his high Consideration.

    (Signed) MALMESBURY.

Lisle, 24th July, 1797.

(No. 27.) Extract of a Dispatch from Lord Malmesbury to Lord Grenville, dated Lisle, Sunday, August 6th, 1797.

My Lord,

I fully expected, when I received the inclosed Note on Friday, that the Conference proposed was to acquaint me with the Instructions the French Plenipotentiaries had received from the Directory, on the Note I had given in near a Fortnight ago, as an Answer to that in which the Restitution of the Whole of His Majesty's Conquests from each of His Enemies is required as an indispensable Preliminary to all Negotiation.

I was therefore surprised and disappointed, when I had taken my Place at the Conference, to hear from the French Plenipotentiaries that the Letters they had

had received that Morning from Paris did not bring any specifick Reply to my last Note, but only went to inform them that the Directory had taken the Subject into their most serious Consideration, and would acquaint them as soon as possible with the Result.

I could not avoid expressing my Concern and Surprise that there existed any Hesitation whatever in the Mind of the Directory on a Point, which, although a very important, was certainly a very simple one:—That to allow it to remain in Doubt whether His Majesty was to have any Compensation or not, was in other Words to leave it in Doubt whether the Directory sincerely meant Peace or not:—And that, although I was very far from wishing for any improper Haste, or not to move in a Matter of such Magnitude without becoming Prudence and Deliberation, yet I could not forbear lamenting that more than a Month had now elapsed without our having advanced a single Step, notwithstanding His Majesty had, in the very Outset of the Negotiation, manifested a Moderation and Forbearance unprecedented under similar Circumstances:—That anxious as I was not to prejudice it by any Representations of mine, I must say, this Delay placed me in a very aukward Position, as I really did not perceive how I could account for it in a Way at all satisfactory, at the same Time that it was quite impossible for me to suffer a longer Space of Time to pass over without writing to my Court.

One of the French Plenipotentiaries expressed his earnest Wish that I would write immediately; he was confident this Delay would be seen in its true light; and added, " Si nous n'avançons pas à pas de Géant, " j'espére que nous marchons d'un pas sur."—And another of them repeated this Phrase.

I expressed my sincere Hope this might be the Case, but it would have been much better proved by the Communication of the Counter Project they had

in

in a Manner pledged themselves to procure, than by any vague and indeterminate Assurances of what might possibly be the Result of the present Suspension of all Business. They observed to me, that the Counter Project would of course be (virtually) contained in their next Instructions, and that their only Motive for wishing to see me was, to convince me that this Delay had neither originated with them, nor been occasioned at Paris by any Want of Attention to this important Business, or from any Cause not immediately and closely connected with it.

I desired to know from them when they thought it probable they should receive positive and explicit Instructions, whether in Three, Four, or Five Days? They said, it would be probably Eight or Ten. And *one of them* observed, that as our not meeting more frequently gave Rise to many idle Rumours and false Reports, he would propose to me, if I had no Obejection, to meet every other Day at Two o'clock: That it was very possible that in our next Two or Three Meetings we might have nothing material to say, but that we should get better acquainted with each other, and in our Conversations mutually suggest Ideas which might be of Use.—I readily consented to this.

I had a Confederate again this Morning. As I was very desirous of being enabled to transmit to your Lordship some more satisfactory Account as to the Motives of this Delay, I again pressed the French Plenipotentiaries on this Point. Each of them repeated what they had said before, and on my endeavouring to make them feel how impossible it was that His Majesty should not be hurt at this Demur on so very simple a Point, *One of them* said, you ought to augur favourably from it; your Note was a Refusal to agree to what was stated by the Directory in their Instructions to us as a *sine quâ non*: If the Directory were determined to persist in this *sine quâ non*, they would have said so at once—" Je
" vous

" vous assure qu'il nous auroit promptement renvoyé *le*
" Courier," were his words:—The Time they took
to deliberate indicates beyond a Doubt that they are
looking for some Temperament, and it scarce can
be doubted that one will be found.—I said I was
well pleased to hear him say this; but that still he
must be aware that it would not be an easy Task for
me to make my Dispatches To-day either interesting
or satisfactory.

Another of the French Ministers said that he really
believed that this would be the only great Impediment we should have to encounter, that every Thing
would go on quickly and smoothly, and that I must
admit the present to be a very important and difficult
Point in the Negotiation. I agreed with him entirely
as to its Importance, but could not acquiesce as to
its Difficulty.

I am very sorry, my Lord, that in such a Moment, and after waiting so long, I should not be
able to send you more explicit and decisive Assurances; but it is not in my Power to compel the
French Negotiators to move on faster. All I can
do is by my Conduct and Language to take care that
no Part whatever of the Imputation of Delay should
attach to me. I have, at every Conference I have
held, always declared my Readiness, to proceed, and
I shall not fail to repeat this every Time we meet.

Right Honourable Lord Grenville, &c. &c. &c.

(No. 28.) Note from the French Plenipotentiaries to Lord Malmesbury.

Les Ministres Plenipotentiaires de la Republique
Françoise seroient charmés de Pouvoir s'entretenir
quelques Instans avec Lord Malmesbury; ils ont en
consequence l'Honneur de lui proposer une Réunion
qui auroit Lieu aujourd'hui à Deux Heures ou à telle
autre qui lui conviendroit mieux, et qu'il voudroit
bien indiquer.

C'est

C'est avec Plaisir qu'ils renouvellent au Lord Malmesbury l'Assurance de leur haute Consideration.

   (Signé) LE TOURNEUR.
         HUGUES B. MARET.

Lille, 17 Thermidor,
An 5me de la Republique.

   COLCHEN, Sec. Gen. de la Legation.

(No. 28.)   Translation.

THE Ministers Plenipotentiary of the French Republick will be happy to have an Opportunity of conversing for a few Minutes with Lord Malmesbury; and they have in consequence the Honor of proposing to him to meet them at Two o'Clock To-day, or at any other Hour which may be more convenient to him, and which he will have the Goodness to appoint.

They renew, with Pleasure, to Lord Malmesbury, the Assurances of their high Confideration.

   (Signed) LE TOURNEUR.
         HUGUES B. MARET.

Lille, 17 Thermidor,
5th Year of the Republick.
 (August 4, 1797.)

     COLCHEN Sec. Gen. of the
     Legation of the Republick.
     (Aug. 4, 1797.)

(No. 29.) Extract of a Dispatch from Lord Malmesbury to Lord Grenville, dated Lille, August 14th, 1797.

My Lord,

IN consequence of the Resolution we had come to, to meet on the Days of the Arrival of the Post from Paris, our Conferences for this last Week have taken place regularly every other Morning, except on Thursday the 10th of August, which
             being

being the Anniverſary of One of their National Feſtivals, the French Legation could not attend.

I have in mine, No. 17, given your Lordſhip an Account of every Thing which paſſed in theſe Conferences, up to that of the 6th. On the 8th nothing was ſaid at all worth tranſmitting, except an Intimation flung out by by *One of the French Plenipotentiaries*, that it would be neceſſary to take into Conſideration the Rights of Neutral Nations on this Occaſion. But as he ſpoke very vaguely, and in general Terms, I did not chooſe to preſs him for an Explanation, as I conſider it more judicious to avoid Diſcuſſions on ſeparate and collateral Points, and not to enter into Negotiation till the Whole can be brought under Deliberation at once.

What paſſed on the 12th was rather more intereſting. The Return of Mr. Weſley afforded me a very natural Opportunity of expreſſing the Impatience with which an Anſwer to my laſt Note was expected by my Court; that Three Weeks had now elapſed ſince its Tranſmiſſion, and that although I by no Means wiſhed to inſinuate that due Attention had not been paid to ſo very important a Subject as that on which we were treating, yet I could not but greatly lament, that Day after Day ſhould be allowed to paſs away without our proceeding at all in the great Buſineſs for which we were met. *One of the French Miniſters* ſaid, That it was impoſſible I could lament this Delay more than they did; that they had already declared to me that it was occaſioned by a Wiſh not to create but to remove Difficulties; and they could aſſure me poſitively, that the French Government had no other Object in View, and that I ſhould find, when once we began fairly to negotiate, we ſhould proceed very rapidly.

I replied it was indeed very material to make good the Time we had loſt. *The French Miniſter* anſwered, you would not call it Time loſt if you knew how it was employed. On my expreſſing, by my Manner, a Wiſh a Wish to be informed, he went on, by saying we will not scruple to tell you, though we feel we ought not yet to do it officially, that we are consulting with our Allies; that we have communicated to them all that has passed here; we have stated that, unless they mean to continue the War, they must release us from our Engagements, and enable us, to a certain Degree, to meet your Proposals.

The Conference of To-day is this Moment over. *One of the French Plenipotentiaries* informed me, that he had received this Morning a Letter from the President of the Directory, assuring him that in Four or Five Days they would receive their final Instructions; and he added of himself, that he trusted these would be such as would enable us to continue our Work without any further Interruption. I said, I hoped these Instructions would be in Substance a Counter Project, as I did not see how any Thing short of One could enable us to proceed so rapidly as he described. He agreed with me entirely, and assured me, that both he and his Colleagues had repeatedly stated the Necessity of a Counter Project being sent them; and he observed, that he really thought the French Government might have foreseen every Thing which had passed, and been prepared with one; and that this would have saved a great deal of valuable Time. As I could not myself have said more, I readily gave a full Assent to what I heard.

(No. 30.)   Extract of a Dispatch from Lord Grenville to Lord Malmesbury, dated Downing Street, August 19th, 1797.

An Expression mentioned in One of your Lordship's last Dispatches to have fallen from One of the French Plenipotentiaries, leads to the Presumption that it is intended, on the Part of France, to bring forward some Proposal about the Navigation of Neutral Powers in Time of War. Your Lordship will best judge of the proper Opportunity of expressing

His

His Majesty's decided and unalterable Resolution on this Point, not to admit of any Proposal for treating with his Enemies on the Subject of the Rights or Claims of Neutral Powers.

The only Remark with which I have to trouble your Lordship by this Messenger, relates to an Expression in the late Message of the Directory to the Council of Five Hundred, which, if literally taken, conveys an accusation against His Majesty's Government, that some Delay has arisen on the Part of this Country in the Negotiations at Lisle. This is so avowedly contrary to the Fact, that it must be considered as impossible that such a Charge could be intended to be made by a Government which had at that Moment delayed for Three Weeks making any Answer to His Majesty's distinct and liberal Proposals of Peace, and whose Plenipotentiaries were daily apologizing to your Lordship for this unbecoming, and as they almost confess, unaccountable Delay; but as the Point is too important to be left unnoticed, it is the King's Pleasure that your Lordship should present a Note, remarking upon the Sense to which these Words are liable, expressing your Persuasion that such cannot be the Intention with which they were used, but asking on the Part of your Court an Explanation to that Effect, which cannot be refused without a Violation of every Thing which Truth and Justice require on such an Occasion.

(No. 31.)   Extract from the Message of the French Directory to the Council of Five Hundred, August 9th, 1797.

En fin, cette Cause est dans le Desespoir où sont tous les vrais Citoyens, et particulierement les Defenseurs de la Patrie, de voir s'eloigner, au Moment même de sa Conclusion, et après l'avoir achetée par tant de Sang et de Souffrance, une Paix Definitive, que sollicitoient enfin avec Empressement les Chefs de la Coalition vaincue, et qu'un Gouvernement,

Ami

Ami de l'Humanité, cherchoit à conclure avec plus d'Empreſſement encore, lorſque, tout à coup, ranimant leurs Eſperances, comptant ſur une Diſſolution générale par le Defaut de Finances, ſur la Deſtruction de Gouvernement, ſur la Mort, ou l'Exil des plus braves Généraux, et ſur la Diſperſion et la Perte des Armées, ces mêmes Puiſſances coaliſées ont mis autant de Lenteur dans les Negotiations, qu'elles avoient montré d'Ardeur pour terminer.

(No. 31.)   Tranſlation.

IN ſhort this Cauſe is in the ſame Deſpondency in which all good Citizens, and particularly the Defenders of the Country are, at ſeeing deferred at the very Moment when its Concluſion was thought to be near at hand, and after having bought it with ſo much Blood and ſo much Suffering—a definitive Peace with the Heads of the vanquiſhed Coalition at length ſolicited in good Earneſt, when its Concluſion was expected, and which a Government, friendly to Humanity, were ſtill more earneſt to conclude: When, all on a ſudden, buoyed up with new Hopes, reckoning upon a general Diſſolution of the Government by the falling of its Finances, upon its Deſtruction, upon the Death or Baniſhment of its braveſt Generals, and upon the Diſperſion and Loſs of its Armies, theſe very ſame coaleſced Powers have thrown as much Delay into the Negotiations, as they had ſhewn Anxiety to bring them to an End.

(No. 32.)   Copy of a Diſpatch from Lord Malmſbury to Lord Grenville, dated Liſle, Auguſt 22, 1797.

My Lord,

IN my Conference of this Morning, I took an Opportunity of remarking to the French Plenipotentiaries on the very unfair and extraordinary Aſſertion which had appeared in the Meſſage of the 9th Inſtant, from the Directory to the Council of Five Hundred,

viz.

viz, "que les Puissances coalisées ont mis autant de Lenteur dans les Negotiations, qu'elles avoient montré de l'Ardeur pour les terminer." I observed to them that I had Orders from my Court to ask a precise Explanation, whether this Accusation of Delay was meant to apply to the Manner in which His Majesty had conducted the Negotiation at Lisle, and if it was so meant, to declare that no Accusation was ever more destitute of Foundation, nor a wider Deviation from the real Fact. I said I was perfectly ready to abide by their Determination on this Point, convinced that it was impossible for them not to acknowledge that the Delay (if there had been any blameable Delay) rested with the French Government and not with His Majesty. The French Plenipotentiaries admitted this to be most strictly true; that the Phrase I had quoted was an ill judged one, and *mal redigée*; but that it could not in any Point of View whatever be construed as applying to England; and they were ready to say, that when it was written, the Directory alluded solely to the Court of Vienna; that they could assure me they had been very faithful in their Reports, and that when they said this it was saying in other Words, that I had carried on the Negotiation with as much Expedition as possible, and that if it had proceeded slowly for this last Month, the Slowness arose on their Side and not on mine.

I said I could not for an Instant call in question their Feelings on this Point; it was the Insinuation conveyed in the Message, and which had gone over Europe, that it was necessary for me to clear up, and to know whether the Directory thought and felt as they did. *One of the French Ministers*, with very strong Expressions, assured me the Directory certainly did think and feel like them; that no unfair or insidious Allusion was meant, and added, "que ce Message etoit fait pour stimuler les Conseils." I went on by observing it was very essential for me to have this fully explained, and that I should give them in a Note to this Effect; they requested I would not, it would lead to disagreeable Discussions, and would not answer the End I proposed. They would take upon themselves *now* to assure me in the Name of the Directory that nothing at all similar to the Construction I put on the Phrase was intended, and that as soon as they could receive an Answer to the Report they should make of To-day's Conversation, they would say the same from the Directory itself.

I hope, my Lord, I have, therefore, by obtaining this very precise and formal Disavowal of an Intention to fix any Imputation of Delay on His Majesty's Government, fulfilled the Object of my Instructions on this particular Point. If when the French Plenipotentiaries speak from the Directory, the Disavowal should not be equally satisfactory and complete, I then will not fail, according to your Lordship's Order, to give in a Note.

I have the Honor to be, &c.
(Signed) MALMESBURY.
Right Honourable Lord Grenville.

(No. 33.)   Extract of a Dispatch from Lord Malmesbury to Lord Grenville, dated Lisle, August 22, 1797.

THE Four Conferences I have held with the French Plenipotentiaries, since I last wrote to your Lordship on the 14th instant, will not, I fear, furnish very interesting Materials for a Dispatch.

Our Conference of this Morning was principally employed in what I have related in my other Dispatch; but the French Plenipotentiaries assured me, that by Thursday, or at the latest by Saturday, they expected to receive their long expected Messenger.

(No. 34.)   Extract of a Dispatch from Lord Malmesbury to Lord Grenville, dated Lisle, August 29, 1797.

I AM extremely sorry to be forced to announce to

your Lordship, that fresh Delays occur in the Progress of the Negociation.

The French Plenipotentiaries informed me at our Conference Yesterday, that the last Answer from Holland was so unsatisfactory that the Directory had ordered the Minister for Foreign Affairs to return it to the Dutch Ministers at Paris; that the Dutch Ministers could not take upon themselves to alter it in the Way the Directory proposed, but had been obliged to refer to their Government for new Orders; and that therefore, supposing no Time to be lost in Deliberation on this Subject at the Hague, it would be at least a Week from To day before any farther Account could be received here.

After lamenting this unexpected Procrastination of our Business, I expressed a Wish to know what the Dutch Answer had been, what Objections the Directory had made to it, and the Alteration they were desirous it should undergo.

One of the French Plenipotentiaries said, it had not been communicated to them, but that he understood it was *complexe, louche, et peu satisfaisante*.—That the Directory expected it should be clear and distinct, and such an one as would enable them to send such Instructions here, as would allow us to go on with the Negotiations in a Way to recover the Time we had lost.

(No. 35.)   Extract of a Dispatch from Lord Malmesbury to Lord Grenville, dated Lisle, September, 5, 1797.

My Lord,

I SHOULD have considered what has passed in our Conferences since I last had the Honour of writing to your Lordship by Mr. Wesley, as in itself too unimportant to authorize me to dispatch a Messenger, but that in general I think it my Duty never to leave your Lordship more than a Week without hearing from me; and I was also glad of an Opportunity

to

to acknowledge the Receipt of your Lordship's Dispatch, No. 23, which was delivered to me by the Messenger Shaw, on the 31st August, at 10. P. M.

Nothing but common Conversation passed in our Conferences of the 30th August and of the 1st September. In that of the 3d the French Plenipotentiaries confirmed what they had taken upon themselves to assure me on the 22d August, in consequence of the Representation I had your Lordship's Orders to make on the Expressions employed by the Directory in their Message of the 9th August to the Councils, and which Expressions appeared to fix an Imputation of Delay on His Majesty's Government, in the Progress of the Negotiation. They said that they had reported to the Directory what I observed on this Subject, and that they were now charged to repeat what I had already heard from them, and to declare that no Intention similar to that I supposed ever existed on the Part of the Directory.

In our Conference of this Morning, although I had Reason to expect that the Answer from the Hague was arrived at Paris, yet it was not admitted by the French Plenipotentiaries.

(No. 36.) Extract of a Dispatch from Lord Malmesbury to Lord Grenville, 9th September, 1797.

I NEED not say that the Two Conferences which have been held since I dispatched the Messenger, Brooks, were not likely, under the present Circumstances of this Country, to afford any Thing extremely important or interesting.

In That of Thursday the 7th, *One of the French Plenipotentiaries* began, on my entering the Room, by announcing a Wish that the great Event which had taken place at Paris, should not interrupt for a long Time our Negotiation, or destroy the pleasing Prospect we had of its soon terminating successfully; and from his Manner I clearly saw he ment to convey the

Idea that it was his Opinion it would not. I endeavoured to difcover whether he fpoke in confequence of any private Inteligence he had received from Paris, or fimply from his own private Judgement, and I found it was entirely from the latter.

In our Conference of this Morning, he faid they were ftill without any Letters from M. Talleyrand (which rather furprifed him); but he could affure me, *with Certainty*, that by Monday they fhould be empowered to go on with the Negotiation, and that I might fafely fay fo to my Court.

(No. 37.)   Extract of a Difpatch from Lord Grenville to Lord Malmefbury, dated Downing Street, September 11th, 1797.

YOUR Lordfhip's Difpatches by the Meffenger, Shaw, were received here this Morning.

It would be premature in the prefent Moment, to enter into any reafoning on the Effect which the extraordinary Events at Paris may be expected to have on the important Negotiation with which your Lordfhip is charged. A very few Days muft now probably fhew, in the moft unequivocal Manner, what are the Views which are entertained by the now predominant Party at Paris, refpecting the Queftion of Peace or War with Great Britain: And it becomes His Majefty's Government to wait the Event with the fame Defire for Accomodation on reafonable Terms, and the fame Firmnefs, with refpect to undue and infulting Demands, which has actuated every Part of the Conduct held by your Lordfhip.

(No. 38.)   Copy of a Difpatch from Lord Malmefbury to Lord Grenville, dated Lifle, Monday, September 11, 1797.

My Lord,

ON my going to the Conference this Morning, the French Plenipotentiaries informed me that the whole
French

French Legation was recalled, and that Meſſrs. Treilhard and Bonnier d'Alco were appointed in their Room. They ſaid, their Orders were to communicate this Event to me immediately, and at the ſame Time to add, in the Name of the French Government, that this Alteration, in the Choice of the Negotiators, <u>would not produce any whatever in the Diſpoſition of the Directory</u>, to bring the Negotiation to a happy Iſſue.

I aſſured them I was extremely ſorry to hear that they were recalled. That we had hitherto acted together ſo cordially, that it was to be lamented any Circumſtances had ariſen which made the French Government think it adviſable to put the Negotiation into other Hands.

That I received with Satisfaction what they told me as to the Sentiments manifeſted by the Directory, relative to the Negotiation, and that I could aſſure them, they were ſuch as certainly exiſted in the Breaſt of my Royal Maſter.

I then ſuggeſted to them, whether it would not be proper to give me an Official Note on this Occaſion, ſince it made a very marked Period in the Negotiation; and as they perfectly agreed with me on the Propriety of this, they ſent me that I now encloſe.

I conſider this Event as ſo material, that I do not loſe a Moment in diſpatching One of my Servants to England, as I have at preſent no Meſſenger with me.

   I have the Honour to be. &c.
    (Signed) MALMESBURY.

Right Honourable Lord Grenville.

(No. 39.) Note from the French Plenipotentiaries to Lord Malmeſbury.

Les Miniſtres Plenipotentiaires de la Republique Françoiſe ont l'Honneur d'informer Lord Malmeſbury qu'ils ont reçu, par l'Ordinarie de ce Jour, un Arrêté
              du

du Directorie Executif, qui porte leur Rappel, et la Nomination des C. C. Treilhard et Bonnier pour leur succeder, et suivre les Négotiations commencées avec l'Angleterre.—Le Ministre des Relations Exterieures, en envoyant aux Ministres Plénipotentiaires soussignés cet Arrêté du Directoire du Vingt-deux de ce Mois, leur mande d'attendre l'Arrivée de leurs Successeurs. Il les charge aussi de prevenir le Ministre Plenipotentiaire de Sa Majesté Britannique que le Changement des Négociateurs n'en apporte aucun dans les Dispositions du Directorie pour la Négotiation.

Les Ministres Plénipotentiaires de la République Françoise ont l'Honneur de réitérer au Lord Malmesbury l'Assurance de leur haute Consideration.

  (Signé) LE TOURNEUR.
     HUGUES B. MARET.

Lille, le 25 Fructidor,
An 5 de la Republique.

  COLCHEN, Sec. Gen. de la Legation.

(No. 40.)   Note from Lord Malmesbury to the French Plenipotentiaries.

Le Ministre Plénipotentiaire de Sa Majesté Britannique a l'Honneur d'accuser la Reception de la Note que les Ministres Plénipotentiaires de la République Françoise lui ont adressée, pour lui faire Part de l'Arrêté du Directoire Exécutif qui porte leur Rappel et la Nomination des Ministres destinés à leur succéder, et à suivre les Negociations déjà commencées. Il reçoit en même tems avec Satisfaction, et transmettra de suite à sa Cour, l'Assurance que ce Changement des Negociateurs n'en apporte aucun dans les Dispositions du Directoire pour la Negociation.

Le Lord Malmesbury, en remerciant les Ministres Plenipotentiaries de la République Françoise de cette Communication, les prie d'être persuadés de ses Regrets personels à l'Occasion de leur Depart, et d'agréer les Assurances de sa haute Consideration.

  (Signé) MALMESBURY.

à Lille, ce 12 September, 1797.

(No. 39.) Tranſlation.

The Miniſters Plenipotentiary of the French Republic have the Honour to inform Lord Malmeſbury that they have received, by this Day's Poſt, a Decree of the Executive Directory, ſignifying their Recall, and the Nomination of Citizens Treilhard and Bonnier to ſucceed them, and to continue the Negotiations entered upon with England.

The Miniſter for Foreign Affairs, in ſending to the Underſigned Miniſters Plenipotentiary this Decree of the Directory, of the 22d of this Month, orders them to wait the Arrival of their Succeſſors. It alſo directs them to inform the Miniſter Plenipotentiary of His Britannick Majeſty, that the Change of the Negotiators does not carry with it any Change in the Diſpoſition of the Directory, with regard to the Negotiation.

The Miniſters Plenipotentiary of the French Republick have the Honour to renew to Lord Malmeſbury the Aſſurances of their high Conſideration.

(Signed) LE TOURNEUR.
HUGUES B. MARET.

Liſle, 25 Fructidor,
5th Year of the Republick.
(Sept.) 11, 1797.)

COLCHEN, Sec. Gen. of the Legation.

(No. 40.) Tranſlation.

The Miniſter Plenipotentiary of His Britannick Majeſty has the Honour to acknowledge the Receipt of the Note which the Miniſters Plenipotentiary of the French Republick have addreſſed to him, communicating the Decree of the Executive Directory, which ſignifies their Recall and the Nomination of the Miniſters deſtined to ſucceed them, and to continue the Negotiations already commenced. He receives at the ſame Time with Satisfaction, and will tranſmit without Delay to his Court, the Aſſurance,

ance, that this Change of the Negotiators does not bring with it any Change in the Difpofition of the Directory as to the Negotiation

Lord Malmefbury in thanking the Minifters Plenipotentiary of the French Republick for this Communication, begs them to be perfuaded of his perfonal Regret on account of their Departure, and to accept the Affurances of his high Confideration.

(Signed) MALMESBURY.

Lifle, Sept. 12, 1797.

(No. 41.)   Extract of a Difpatch from Lord Malmefbury to Lord Grenville, dated Lifle, 17th September, 1797.

My Lord,

The new French Plenipotentiaries, Meffieurs Treilhard and Bonnier d'Alco, with their principal Secretary M. Derché, and Two private Secretaries, arrived here at Five o'Clock A. M. on Wednefday the 13th Inftant. At Eleven A. M. they fent M. Derché to acquaint me with their Arrival, and to inquire at what Hour I would receive their Vifit. In confequence of my faying whenever it was convenient to them, they came immediately, attended by Meffieurs Le Tourneur, Maret, and Colchen.

On taking Leave, M. Le Tourneur came forward and faid to me, in his Name and that of his Colleagues, that they could not terminate their Miffion without expreffing the Satisfaction they had felt from the Opennefs and Candour (Loyauté et Franchife) with which I had acted during the Whole of the Negotiation, or take Leave of me, without expreffing their fincere perfonal Regrets; that the Recollection of my Conduct would always be agreeable to them, and that it had given me the ftrongeft Title to their Efteem and good Wifhes.

After giving the new Plenipotentiaries as much Time as was neceffary to return to their own Houfe, I fent Mr. Rofs to afk at what Hour I might return

their

their Visit; and, in consequence of their Answer, I went to them, attended by Lord Morpeth and Mr. Ellis.

I took an Opportunity of returning the Compliment M. Le Tourneur had made me; and I must in Justice repeat my Lord, what I have already said, that his Conduct and that of his Colleagues has, in every Point which has depended on them, been perfectly fair and honorable, and in no Instance contrary to the Principles they announced, and the Professions they made. It is therefore impossible for me not to regret them, and not to consider the Change of Negotiators at least as a very unpleasant, if not a very unfortunate Incident.

(No. 42.) Copy of a Dispatch from Lord Malmesbury to Lord Grenville, dated Lisle, 17th September, 1797.

My Lord,

I SHALL endeavour in this Dispatch to give your Lordship as circumstantial an Account as my Memory will allow me to do, of what has passed in the Two Conferences I have held with the new French Plenipotentiaries.

In that of Friday the 14th, after communicating to me the Arrêté of the Directory appointing them to succeed Messieurs Le Tourneur and Maret, and empowering them to continue the Negotiation with me, *One of them* began by making the strongest Assurances of the sincere Desire entertained by the Directory for Peace. He observed, that if this Desire had manifested itself so strongly at a Moment when the Two great Authorities of the Country were at Variance, it must naturally become stronger and be exerted with more Effect when all spirit of Division was suppressed, and when the Government was strengthened by the perfect Concord which now reigns between all its Branches: That the first and most material Point to be ascertained in every Negotiation

tiation was the <u>Extent of the full Powers</u> with which the Negotiators are vested; that I should find theirs to be very ample: and that, as it was necessary to the Success of our Discussions that mine should be equally so, they had it in Command to present a Note, the Object of which was to inquire, "whether <u>I was authorized to treat on the Principle of a general Restitution</u> of every Possession remaining in His Majesty's Hands, not only belonging to them, but to their Allies; that I was not unacquainted with their Laws and with their Treaties; that a great Country could not on any Occasion act in Contradiction to them; and that, aware as I must be of this, I could not but expect the Question contained in the Note, neither could I consider the Requisition of <u>an explicit Answer, previous to entering upon the Negotiation</u>, as arising from any other Motive than that of the most perfect Wish, on the Part of the Directory, to bring it to a successful, and, above all, to a speedy Conclusion.

I replied, that if after what I heard I could allow myself to hope for such an Event as he seemed to think probable, or give any Credit to the pacifick Dispositions he announced on the Part of the French Government, such Hope must arise solely from the Confidence I might place in his Assurances; since the Measure itself now adopted by the Directory was certainly calculated to make a directly contrary Impression on my Mind; that I could not conceal from him, that far from expecting such a Question, its being now put surprized me beyond Measure, and still more so, when from his Comment upon it I was to infer, that he wished me to consider it as tending to promote a speedy Pacification; that the Question expressed in the Note he had delivered (for he had given it to me, and I had read it over as he ended his Speech) was Word for Word the same as that put to me by his Predecessors so long ago as the 14th July; that on the

15th

15th I had, from my own Authority, given an Answer, and that this Answer I confirmed fully and distinctly by Order of my Court on the 24th July; that these Notes had to the present Hour remained unnoticed, and a delay of Two Months had occurred; that the Reasons assigned for this Delay were, as I was repeatedly told, a decided Resolution on the Part of the French Government to listen to the reasonable Proposals made by His Majesty; but that being bound by their Engagements with the Court of Madrid and the Batavian Republick, and wishing to treat their Allies with due Consideration, they were desirous of Consulting with them previous to any positive Declaration, and obtaining from them a voluntary Release from those Engagements sufficient to enable the French Plenipotentiaries here to admit the Basis His Majesty had established, and to ground on it all future Discussions which might arise in the Course of the Negotiation; that if he had read over the Papers left, undoubtedly, in his Possession by his Predecessors, he would find what I stated to be strictly true; and that of course it could not be difficult to account for my Surprize, when, after being told that he and his Colleague were to take up the Negotiation precisely where they found it, it now became evident that it was to be flung back to the very Point from which we started, and flung back in a Way which seemed to threaten a Conclusion very different from that he foretold.

I shall not attempt to follow *the French Minister* through the very elaborate and certainly able Speech he made in Reply, with a View to convince me that the Enquiry into the Extent of my Full-Powers was the strongest Proof the Directory could furnish of their pacifick Intention, and the shortest Road they could take to accomplish the desired End. It was in order to give Activity to the Negotiation, (*activer* was his Word), and to prevent its stagnating, that this Demand was made so specifically; and he

inti-

intimated to me, that it was impossible for the Directory to proceed till a full and satisfactory Answer had been given to it. I interrupted him here, by saying, their Manner of acting appeared to me calculated to decide the Negotiation at once, not to give it Activity, since it must be known, I could not have Powers of the Description he alluded to; and even supposing I had, the admitting it would be in Fact neither more or less than a compleat Avowal of the Principle itself, which once agreed on, nothing would be left to negotiate about. *The other French Plenipotentiary* interposed here, by saying, *that would not be the Case; many Articles would still remain to be proposed, and many Points for important Discussion.* I said, every Word I heard seemed to present fresh Difficulties. Without replying to me, the *first-mentioned Minister* went on by endeavouring to prove, "that the Avowal of having Powers to a certain Extent, did not imply the Necessity of exercising them; that it was the Avowal alone for which they contended, in order to determine at once the Form the Negotiation was to take; that the Note, and the Time prescribed in it, were in consequence of the most positive Orders from the Directory; and that if I drew from it a Conclusion different from the Assurances they had made me in the Name of the Directory, I did not make the true Inference." I replied, that, although the prescribing the Day on which the Question was to put me as the Term within which I was to give my Answer to it, was both a very unusual and abrupt Mode of proceeding, yet as a Day was much more than sufficient for the Purpose, I should forbear making any particular Remark on this Circumstance: That as to the Inference to be drawn from the positive Manner in which they appeared to maintain the Question put to me, I really could not make it different from that I had already expressed: That the reverting, after an Interval of Two Months, to a Question already answered, and which Question

involved

involved the Fate of the Negotiation, certainly could not be confidered as wearing a very conciliatory Appearance: That in regard to my Anfwer, it could not be different from that I had given before: That my full Powers, which were in their Hands, were as extenfive as any could be, and it did not depend on me to give them more or lefs Latitude; but that in fact their Queftion went not to the Extent of my full Powers, but to require of me to declare the Nature of my Inftructions; and on this Point they certainly would forgive me if I did not fpeak out till fuch Time as the Circumftances of the Negotiation called upon me to do it.

The French Minifter ftrove to prove to me, what he had before attempted, that the claiming a Right of Enquiry into the Nature of the difcretionary Authority confided in a Minifter, by no Means implied an Intention of requiring of him to act up to it to its utmoft Limits. I obferved, if no fuch Intention exifted, why inftitute the Enquiry? and if it did exift, why not fay fo at once?—*He* faid, what we now afk is little more than a Matter of Form; when you have given us your Anfwer, we fhall follow it up by another Step, which we are ordered to take. I faid, my Anfwer was given Two Months ago; that, although I was ready to give it them again, and in Writing, as One to their Note, yet, as it could not be different, I did not fee why they fhould not proceed immediately to the other Step, by which I was told the Qeftion was to be followed up. It would be premature, faid *the French Minifter*; but in drawing up your Anfwer, do not forget the Force of the Arguments I have ufed, or in your Report to your Court, the Affurances we have given of the earneft Wifh of the Directory to terminate the War.

I replied, that I ftill muft maintain, that from the Manner in which they thought proper to define full Powers, I could fee no Diftinction between acknowledging the Power and admitting the Principle;

and

and that the Question itself could not be put with any other Intention—(Your Lordship will observe, from the subsequent Notes which passed between us, that I was perfectly grounded in this Assertion);— that in my Reports, they might be fully assured I should act up to that conciliatory Spirit, which, from the earliest Period of the Negotiation, had always decided my Conduct; and that, inauspicious as Appearances were, I certainly would be careful not to make them look *hostile*. At the Word hostile, both the French Plenipotentiaries were most warm in their Protestations, that nothing could be less so; that the Idea of the Negotiation breaking off was as far from their Thoughts as from their Wishes. I said, that although I heard this with Pleasure, yet I could not avoid adverting to Facts, and that, when instead of an Answer, and the favourable Answer which I had every Reason to expect, I received only the Repetition of a Demand, which had been already satisfied Two Months ago; I certainly could not think this a good Omen. If it did not bode an immediate Rupture of the Treaty, it assuredly did not announce a near and successful Termination of it. *The above-mentioned Minister* persisted I was mistaken; that the Business would end speedily; that Speed was their Wish, and Speed with Peace for its Object.

On breaking up our Conference, I said, that I took it for granted we should meet again at the usual Hour, on Sunday. *He* said, that it perhaps might not be necessary, but that they certainly would let me know in Time; and this conveyed to me the first Idea of what has since taken place.

I inclose your Lordship the Note A, I received in this Conference from the French Plenipotentiaries, and the Answer B, which I made to it Yesterday Morning at 10 A. M.

At 6 P. M. the Note C was transmitted to me; to which at 8 P. M. I returned the Answer D, by Mr.

Mr. Rofs, whom I sent in order that he might bring me the Passports I asked for; but at a Quarter before 10 P. M. M. Derché, Secretary of the French Legation, delivered to me the Paper marked E; and this Morning at 9 A. M. I replied by the Note F, which immediately produced that marked G.

The Notes sent me by the French Plenipotentiaries speak for themselves; and it is unnecessary to enter into any Reflexions on them. I am willing to hope that the Answers I have made were such as became the Situation in which I stand, the Importance of the Cause intrusted to me, and the steady but temperate Conduct which the Spirit of my Instructions injoin me to hold.

It was my Wish to give every Opening to the French Plenipotentiaries to recal the violent Step they had taken; and, if possible, to convince them of its extreme Impropriety. And it was with this View, and with a most anxious Desire not to exclude all Hope of the Restoration of Peace, that I determined on suggesting the Idea of our meeting once more before I left Lille.

This Meeting took place To-day at Noon: I opened it by observing, That the several Notes they had received from me since the preceding Evening had been too expressive of the Surprize I felt at the Measure the Directory had thought proper to adopt, to make it necessary for me to enlarge upon it in this Conference; and indeed my sole Motive for suggesting that it might be for our mutual Satisfaction that it should be held, was, because this Measure appeared to me to be in such direct Contradiction to the very strong Assurances I had so constantly and repeatedly heard from them, and to the pacifick Intentions with which they declared they were sent, that it was my earnest Wish (before I considered their Conduct as forcing me to a Step which must so materially affect the Success of the Negotiation), to be perfectly certain that I understood clearly and distinctly

distinctly the precise Meaning of their official Notes. On their admitting that nothing could be more reasonable than that I should, on so important a Point, require Explanation, or more satisfactory to them than to give it me (as far as lay in their Power), I proceeded by saying, that it appeared to me that I was called upon to produce immediately my full Powers, or rather my Instructions (for however different these were in themselves, in their Demand they seemed constantly blended), and that if either I refused to consent to this, or if on consenting to it, it was found that I was not authorised to treat on the Principle they laid down, I was then in the Space of Twenty-four Hours to leave Lille, and return to my Court; and that I was required to obtain full Authority to admit this Principle, if it was wished the Negotiation should proceed. This I said appeared to me to be the evident Sense of the Notes, and I begged to know whether I had mistaken it or not. *One of the French Plenipotentiaries* said, " You " have understood it exactly; I hope you equally " understand the Intention of the French Govern- " ment, which is to accelerate Peace by removing " every Obstacle which stands in its Way."

I replied, that having now no Doubt left on my Mind as to their exact Meaning, and being quite sure notwithstanding the Observation they had made, *que j'avais saisi la veritable Intention de leur Note*, it would, I feared, be a very unprofitable Employment of our Time to argue either on the Nature of the Principle they announced as a sine quâ non, to even a preliminary Discussion, or on the extreme Difficulty of reconciling the peremptory Demand with which they opened their Mission, to the pacifick Professions that accompanied it; that if they were determined to persist in this Demand, it was much better to avoid all useless Altercation; and nothing in that Case remained for me to do, but to ask for my Passports, and to signify to them my Intention

of

of leaving France at an early Hour the next Morning. They said, they had their Hands tied by an Arrêté of the Directory, and were bound to obſerve the Conduct they had followed by the moſt poſitive Orders; and although we remained together ſome Time longer, not a Hint dropped from them expreſſive of a Wiſh that, inſtead of going myſelf for new Inſtructions, I ſhould either Write for them by a Meſſenger, or obtain them by ſending to England One of the Gentlemen who are with me. I endeavoured by every indirect Means to ſuggeſt to them the Neceſſity of adopting ſome ſuch Modification, if they meant that their Wiſhes for Peace, in the Expreſſion of which they were this Morning more eager than ever, ſhould meet with the ſlighteſt Degree of Credit: I again brought to their Recollection that I was authorized to receive any Propoſal, any *Contre Projet* they tendered to me, but that they muſt be aware that it was not poſſible for me to alter the Orders I had received, or to aſſume an Authority with which I was not inveſted. I dwelt particularly and repeatedly on my being competent to take any Thing they ſaid for Reference; but this availed nothing, except drawing from *One of them* a Remark, that the full Powers which authorized a Miniſter to hear Propoſals, were widely different from thoſe which would enable him to accede to them; and that it was ſuch full Powers that the Directory required me to ſolicit.

An eaſy Anſwer preſented itſelf to this Mode of Reaſoning; but I ſaw no Advantage to be derived from prolonging a Converſation, which, after the poſitive Declaration they had made, could lead to nothing: I therefore ended the Conference by declaring my Reſolution to begin my Journey at a very early Hour the next Morning, and by ſaying, that immediately on my Arrival in England I would make an exact Report of every Thing that had paſſed ſince their Arrival.

I trust, my Lord, I shall not incur Censure for having declined to offer in distinct Terms to wait at Lille till I could know His Majesty's Pleasure on the peremptory Proposal made to me: But when I considered the Nature of the Proposal itself, the Avowal *that this would not be the last*, nor perhaps the most humiliating, Condition required of us, and the imperious Style with which I was enjoined to depart in Twenty-four Hours, it was utterly impossible for me to assume a Language or affect a Manner that could be interpreted into Solicitation or Entreaty: I felt myself called upon to treat the Whole of this extraordinary Proceeding with Calmness and Temper; and notwithstanding the deep and poignant Concern I must feel at an Event which I fear will remove all Probability of an immediate Pacification, I trust that in the Expression of this Sentiment I have not used a Language unbecoming the Character with which I am invested, or the Greatness of the Sovereign and Country whose Dignity and Interests it is my primary Duty to consult and to maintain.

I have the Honor to be
    with great Respect, my Lord,
        your Lordship's most obedient
           humble Servant,
       (Signed)   MALMESBURY.

Right Honourable Lord Grenville.

(No. 43. A.)   Note from the French Plenipotentiaries to Lord Malmesbury.

Les soussignés Ministres Plenipotentiaires de la Republique Française, chargés de traiter de la Paix avec l'Angleterre, ont l'Honneur d'assurer le Lord Malmesbury, Ministre Plenipotentiaire de Sa Majesté Britannique, que le Gouvernement Français veut aussi sincèrement, aussi fortement que jamais, une Paix desirée par les Deux Nations; mais ne pouvant conclure qu'une Paix basée sur les Loix et les Traités
                                      qui

qui lient la Republique Françaife, perfuadé que pour parvenir à ce But il faut s'expliquer avec une entiere Franchife, et voulant imprimer à la Negotiation la plus grande Activité, le Directoire Executif a expreffement chargé les Souffignés de demander au Lord Malmefbury, s'il a des Pouvoirs fuffifans pour, dans le Traité qui feroit conclu, reftituer à la Republique Françaife et à fes Allies, toutes les Poffeffions qui depuis le Commencement de la Guerre ont paffé dans la Main des Anglais.

Les Souffignés font également chargés par le Directoire Executif de demander au Lord Malmefbury une Reponfe dans le Jour. Ils le prient d'agréer les Temoignages de leur haute Confideration.

    (Signé)   TREILHARD.
           BONNIER.

Lille, le 29 Fructidor,
An 5e de la Republique.

    Par les Miniftres Plenipotentiaires,
    Je Sec. Gen. de la Legation.
           DERCHÉ.

(No. 43. A.)   Tranflation.

THE underfigned Minifters Plenipotentiaries of the French Republick, commiffioned to treat of Peace with England, have the Honour to affure Lord Malmefbury, Minifter Plenipotentiary of His Britannick Majefty, that the French Government wifhes as fincerely, as ftrongly as ever, a Peace, defired by the Two Nations: But, <u>unable to conclude any other Peace than fuch a one as is founded on the Laws and on the Treaties which bind the French Republick</u>, perfuaded that, to arrive at this End, it is neceffary to explain itfelf with entire Franknefs, and defirous of giving to the Negotiation the greateft Rapidity, the Executive Directory has exprefsly charged the Underfigeed <u>to demand of Lord Malmefbury, whether he has fufficient Powers for reftoring,</u>

in

in the Treaty which may be concluded, to the French Republick and to its Allies, all the Poſſeſſions which, ſince the Beginning of the War, have paſſed into the Hands of the Engliſh.

The Underſigned are equally charged by the Executive Directory to demand from Lord Malmeſbury <u>an Anſwer in the Courſe of the Day</u>. They requeſt him to accept the Aſſurances of their high conſideration.

(Signed)   TREILHARD.
BONNIER.

Lille, 29 Fructidor,
5th Year of the Republick.
(Sept. 15, 1797.)

By the Miniſters Plenipotentiary of the French Republick, the Sec. Gen.
DERCHÉ.

(No. 44. B.)   Note from Lord Malmeſbury to the French Plenipotentiaries.

LE ſouſſigné Miniſtre Plenipotentiaire de Sa Majeſté Britannique reçoit avec beaucoup de Satisfaction l'Expreſſion du Deſir ſincere pour la Paix, que les Miniſtres Plenipotentiaires de la Republique Françoiſe lui ont annoncé Hier au Nom de leur Gouvernement. Il a l'Honneur de les aſſurer que le Roi ſon Maitre eſt animé du même Deſir, et n'a rien de plus à Cœur que de mettre Fin aux Malheurs de la Guerre.

Quant à la Queſtion que les Miniſtres Plenipotentiaires de la Republique Françoiſe adreſſent au Lord Malmeſbury ſur l'Etendue de ſes plein Pouvoirs, il croit dejà avoir fait à ce Sujet la Reponſe la moins equivoque dans les Deux Notes qu'il à remiſes à leurs Predeceſſeurs le 15 et le 24 du Mois de Juillet. Cependant, pour eviter toute Meſentendue, Il renouvelle la Declaration qu'il à faite Hier; ſavoir, qu'il ne peut et ne doit traiter que d'après le Principe des Compenſations; Principe qui à été formellement

lement reconnû comme Base d'une Traité egalement juste, honorable, et avantageux aux Deux Puissances.

Le Lord Malmesbury prie les Ministres Plenipotentiaires de la Republique Françoise d'agréer les Assurances de sa haute Consideration.

(Signé) MALMESBURY.

à Lille, ce Samedi, 16 Septembre,
à 10 A. M. 1797.

(No. 44. B.)   Translation.

THE undersigned Minister Plenipotentiary of His Britannick Majesty receives with great Satisfaction the Expression of the sincere Desire for Peace, which the Ministers Plenipotentiaries of the French Republick announced to him Yesterday in the Name of their Government. He has the Honour to assure them that the King his Master is animated with the same Desire, and has nothing more at Heart than to put an End to the Calamities of the War.

With regard to the Question which the Ministers Plenipotentiary of the French Republick addressed to Lord Malmesbury, concerning the Extent of his full Powers, he considers himself as having already given the most unequivocal Answer upon this Subject, in the Two Notes which he delivered to their Predecessors on the 15th and 24th of July.

However, to avoid all misunderstanding, he renews the Declaration, which he made Yesterday; that is to say, that he neither can or ought to treat upon any other Principle than that of Compensations; a Principle which has been formally recognized as the Basis of a Treaty equally just, honourable, and advantageous to the Two Powers.

Lord Malmesbury requests the Ministers Plenipotentiary of the French Republick to accept the Assurances of his high Consideration.

(Signed) MALMESBURY.

Lisle, Saturday, 16th September, 1797.
10 A. M.

(No. 45. C.) Note from the French Plenipotentiaries to Lord Malmesbury.

Les Miniſtres Plenipotentiaires de la Republique Françaiſe chargés de traiter de la Paix avec l'Angleterre, ont l'Honneur d'accuſer la Reception de la Reponſe du Lord Malmeſbury à la Note qui lui a été remiſe dans la Conference d'Hier.

Il reſulte de cette Reponſe et des Deux Notes des 15 & 24 Juillet aux quelles elle ſe refère, que le Lord Malmeſbury n'a pas de Pouvoirs pour conſentir à la Reſtitution de toutes les Poſſeſſions que Sa Majeſté Britannique occupe, ſoit ſur la Republique Françaiſe, ſoit ſur ſes Alliés.

En conſequence, en réiterant au Lord Malmeſbury les Aſſurances les plus poſitives des Sentimens du Gouvernement Français, les Souſſignés lui donnent Connoiſſance d'un Arrêté du Directoire Executif, portant que dans le Cas où Lord Malmeſbury declarera n'avoir pas les Pouvoirs neceſſaries pour conſentir á toutes les Reſtitutions que les Loix et les Traités qui lient la Republique Françaiſe rendent indiſpenſables, il aura à ſe retirer dans les Vingt quatre Heures vers ſa Cour pour demander les Pouvoirs ſuffiſans. Le Lord Malmeſbury ne peut voir dans cette Determination de Directoire Executif qu'une Intention de hâter l'Inſtant où les Negotiations pourront être ſuivies avec la Certitude d'une prompte Concluſion.

Les Miniſtres Plenipotentiaires de la Republique Françaiſe prient le Lord Malmeſbury d'agréer les Aſſurances de leur haute Conſideration.

(Signé)   TREILHARD.
BONNIER.

Lille, 30 Fructidor,
An 5 de la Republique Françaiſe.

Par les Miniſtres Plenipotentiaires,
le Sec. Gen. de la Legation,
DERCHÉ.

No. 45. C.) Translation.

THE Ministers Plenipotentiaries of the French Republick, commissionned to treat of Peace with England, have the Honour to acknowledge the Receipt of the Answer of Lord Malmesbury to the Note which was presented to him in the Conference of Yesterday.

It appears from this Answer, and from the Two Notes of the 15th and 24th of July, to which it refers, that Lord Malmesbury has not Powers for agreeing to the Restitution of all the Possessions which His Britannick Majesty occupies, whether from the French Republick, or from its Allies.

In consequence, while they reiterate to Lord Malmesbury the most positive Assurances of the Sentiments of the French Government, the Undersigned apprize him of a Decree of the Executive Directory, which signifies that, in Case Lord Malmesbury shall declare himself not to have the necessary Powers for agreeing to all the Restitutions which the Laws and the Treaties which bind the French Republick, make indispensable, he shall be to return, in Four-and-twenty Hours, to his Court, to ask for sufficient Powers. Lord Malmesbury can see in this Determination of the Executive Directory nothing else than an Intention to hasten the Moment when the Negociation may be followed up with the Certainty of a speedy Conclusion.

The Ministers Plenipotentiaries of the French Republick request Lord Malmesbury to accept the Assurances of their high Consideration.

(Signed) TREILHARD.
BONNIER.

By the Ministers Plenipotentiaries,
the Sec. Gen. of the Legation,
DERCHÉ.

Lisle, 30 Fructidor, 5th Year of the Republick. (Sept. 16, 1797.)

(No. 46. D.)   Note from Lord Malmesbury to the French Plenipotentiaries.

Le soussigné Ministre Plénipotentiaire de Sa Majesté Britannique a l'Honneur d'accuser la Réception de la Note en Date d'aujourd'hui, qui lui a été remise de la Part des Ministres Plénipotentiaires de la République Française.

Quelque Chagrin qu'il éprouve à voir s'évanouir l'Espoir d'une prompte Conciliation, il ne peut répondre à un Réfus aussi absolu de continuer les Négociations sur les bases qui lui paraissaient déjà arrêtées, qu'en demandant les Passeports nécessaires pour lui et pour sa Suite, afin de pouvoir, dans les Vingt-quatre Heures se mettre en Route, et se rendre de suite en Angleterre.

Il prie les Ministres Plénipotentiaires de la République Française d'agréer les Assurances de sa haute Considération.

           (Signé)   MALMESBURY.

A Lille, ce Samedi, 16 Septembre, à 8 P. M.

(No. 46. D.)   Translation.

The undersigned Minister Plenipotentiary of his Britannick Majesty has the Honour to acknowledge the Receipt of the Note of this Day, which has been sent him by the Ministers Plenipotentiary of the French Republick.

Whatever Regret he may experience at seeing the Hope of a speedy Conciliation thus destroyed, he can return no other Answer to a Refusal so absolute to continue the Negotiation on Grounds which appeared to have been already agreed upon, than by demanding the necessary Passports for himself and his Suite, in Order that they may set off within the Four-and-twenty Hours, and return immediately to England.

He requests the Ministers Plenipotentiary of the French Republick to accept the Assurances of his high Consideration.

           (Signed)   MALMESBURY.

Lisle, Saturday, 16th September, 8 P. M.

(No. 47. E.)   Note from the French Plenipotentiaries to Lord Malmesbury.

Les soussignés Ministres Plénipotentiaires de la République Française chargés de traiter de la Paix avec l'Angleterre, ont l'Honneur d'accuser la Réception de la Réponse de Lord Malmesbury à la Note qu'ils lui ont adressée aujourd'hui.

Ils croient devoir lui observer, qu'il ne paraît pas en avoir saisi la véritable Intention ; qu'elle ne contient nullement un Réfus de continuer les Négociations, mais, au contraire, un Moyen de les activer et de les suivre avec un Succès, aussi désirable pour les Deux Nations qu'il serait Flatteur pour les Ministres chargés de négocier.

Le Gouvernement Français est si éloigné des Intentions que semble supposer la Note du Lord Malmesbury, que les Ministres Plénipotentiaires de la République Française n'ont reçu aucun Ordre de quitter le Lieu des Conférences après le Départ du Ministre Plénipotentiaire de Sa Majesté Britannique.

Les Ministres Plénipotentiaires de la République Française prient le Lord Malmesbury d'agréer les Assurances de leur haute Considération.

          (Signé)   TREILHARD.
                          BONNIER.

Lille, ce 30 Fructidor, an 5 de la République Française.

Par les Ministres Plénipotentiaires,
   le Sec. Gén. de la Légation,
                      DERCHÉ.

(No. 47. E.)   Translation.

The undersigned Ministers Plenipotentiary of the French Republick, commissioned to treat of Peace with England, have the Honour to acknowledge the Receipt of Lord Malmesbury's Answer to the Note which they addressed to him this Day.

They think it right to observe to him, that he does not appear to have seized the real meaning of their Note; that it by no means contains Refusal to continue the Negociations, but, on the contrary, the Means for giving them Activity, and for following them up with a Success, no less desirable to the Two Nations, than it would be flattering to the Ministers charged with the Conduct of them.

The French Government is so far from entertaining the Intentions which the Note of Lord Malmesbury appears to impute to them, that the Ministers Plenipotentiary of the French Republick have received no Order to quit Lisle, after the Departure of the Minister Plenipotentiary of his Britannick Majesty.

The Ministers Plenipotentiary of the French Republick request Lord Malmesbury to accept the Assurances of their high Consideration.

    (Signed) TREILHARD,
            BONNIER.

By the Ministers Plenipotentiary,
 the Sec. Gen. of the Legation,
          DERCHÉ.

Lisle, 30 Fructidor, 5th Year of the French Republick. (Sept. 16, 1797.)

(No. 48. F.)   Note from Lord Malmesbury to the
          French Plenipotentiaries.

LE soussigné Ministre Plénipotentiaire de Sa Majesté Britannique a l'Honneur d'accuser la Réception de la Note que les Ministres Plénipotentiaires de la République Française lui ont transmise Hier au Soir, par les Mains du Sécrétaire Général de leur Légation. Il croit ne pas pouvoir mieux répondre qu'en leur soumettant à son Tour les Observations suivantes.

Qu'ayant déjà fait, par sa Note du 24 Juillet, & d'après les Ordres exprès de sa Cour, une Réponse à la Question qui vient d'être si inopinément renouvellée, Question qui ne portant en Apparence que sur les Limites de ses Plein-pouvoirs (qui sont des plus amples) exige en effet la Déclaration de toute l'Etendue de ses Instructions :—et ne pouvant être autorisé en aucun Cas, hormi celui de la Rupture des Négociations, de quitter le Lieu de sa Destination sans les Ordres exprès du Roi son Maître; il n'a pû regarder une Note portant, d'après un Arrêté du Directoire Exécutif, " qu'il avait à se retirer " dans les Vingt-quatre Heures vers sa Cour," que comme une Démarche peu propre à accélérer la Confection de la Paix.—Cependant, pour répondre aux Assurances des Ministres Plénipotentiaires de la République Française, et pour témoigner son Désir de bien saisir leur véritable Intention, sur laquelle il serait très-fâché de se méprendre, il croit qu'il pourrait être plus satisfaisant de se réunir encore une Fois; et dans le Cas où les Ministres Plénipotentiaires de la République Française se trouvassent du même Avis, le Lord Malmesbury leur proposerait que cette Réunion eût Lieu de meilleure Heure que de Coutume, afin qu'il se trouve à Tems de prendre le Parti que pourra exiger le Résultat de leur Conférence.

Il prie les Ministres Plénipotentiaires de la République Française d'agréer les Assurances de sa haute Considération.

    (Signé) MALMESBURY.

A Lille, ce Dimanche,
17 Septembre 1797.

(No. 48. F.)   Translation.

THE undersigned Minister Plenipotentiary of His Britannick Majesty has the Honour to acknowledge the Receipt of the Note which the Ministers Plenipotentiary of the French Republick transmitted to him Yesterday, through the Hands of the Secretary

Gene-

General of their Legation. He thinks he cannot answer it better than by submitting to them in his Turn the following Observations.

That having already by his Note, dated July 24, and in Obedience to the express Orders of his Court, given an Answer to the Question which is now so unexpectedly renewed, a Question, that in Appearance relates solely to the Limits of his full Powers, (which are in the most ample Form), but which does in Fact require a Declaration of the whole Extent of his Instructions; and not being authorised to quit the Place of his Destination without the express Orders of the King his Master, in any Case except that of the Rupture of the Negociation; he could not help considering a Note enjoining him, in consequence of a Decree of the Executive Directory, to return to his Court in the Space of Four-and-Twenty Hours, as ill calculated to accelerate the Conclusion of Peace: Nevertheless, to answer the Assurances of the Ministers Plenipotentiary of the French Republick, and to testify his Desire to seize their real Meaning, with respect to which he should be very sorry to deceive himself, he thinks that it would be more satisfactory to meet once more; and if the Ministers Plenipotentiary of the French Republick should be of the same Opinion, Lord Malmesbury would propose that this Meeting should take place at an earlier Hour than usual, in order that he may have Time to take such Steps as the Result of their Conference may render necessary. He desires the Ministers Plenipotentiary of the French Republick to accept the Assurances of his high Consideration.

(Signed)   MALMESBURY.

Lisle, Sunday,
Sept. 17, 1797.

(No. 49. G.) Note from the French Plenipotentiaries to Lord Malmesbury.

Les soussignés Ministres Plénipotentiaires de la République Française, chargés de traiter de la Paix avec l'Angleterre, ont l'Honneur d'accuser la Réception de la Note que le Ministre Plénipotentiaire de Sa Majesté Britannique leur a transmise ce Matin. En se référant aux Notes adressées à Lord Malmesbury les 29 et 30 Fructidor, et notamment à la première du Jour d'Hier, ils acceptent la Réunion que le Lord Malmesbury paraît désirer, et lui proposent l'Heure de Midi.

Ils prient le Ministre Plénipotentiaire de Sa Majesté Britannique d'agréer les Assurances de leur haute Considération.

(Signé) TREILHARD.
BONNIER.

Lille, le 1 Jour complémentaire de l'An 5 de la République Française.

Par les Ministres Plénipotentiaires, le Sec. Gén. de la Légation.
DERCHÉ.

(No. 49. G.) Translation.

The undersigned Ministers Plenipotentiary of the French Republick, commissioned to treat of Peace with England, have the Honour to acknowledge the Receipt of the Note which the Minister Plenipotentiary of His Britannick Majesty has transmitted to them this Morning, Referring to the Notes addressed to Lord Malmesbury on the 29th and 30th Fructidor, and especially to the First of Yesterday, they agree to the Meeting which Lord Malmes-

Malmesbury appears to desire, and propose the Hour of Noon.

They request Lord Malmesbury to accept the Assurances of their high Consideration.

(Signed)   TREILHARD.
BONNIER.

Lisle, 1st Complementary Day,
5th Year of the French Republick. (17 Sept. 1797.)

By the Ministers Plenipotentiary,
the Sec. Gen. of the Legation,
DERCHÉ.

(No. 50.)   Dispatch from Lord Grenville to Lord Malmesbury, dated Downing-Street, Sept. 22, 1797.

[handwritten: He in London He arrived there on the Ev:g of the 20th]

My Lord,

I HAVE had the Honour of laying before His Majesty your Lordship's Dispatches, in which you have given an Account of the extraordinary Conduct of the new Plenipotentiaries of the French Republick, of the Answers given by your Lordship to their unjustifiable Demand, and of your consequent Departure from Lisle.

I have the Satisfaction to be able to assure your Lordship that His Majesty has been pleased to express His entire Approbation of your Lordship's judicious and temperate Conduct in the unprecedented Situation in which you were placed, and of the Manner in which you expressed yourself, both in your official Notes, and in your Conversations with the French Plenipotentiaries, as well as of that in which you have conducted yourself during the whole Course of the Negociation, which seems too likely to be now brought to its Close.

As it appears, however, that some further Answer will probably be expected by the French Government to their late extraordinary Demand, notwithstanding

standing the full and conclusive Reply given in your Lordship's Notes, I have received the King's Commands to transmit to you the inclosed Draft of a Note, which it is His Majesty's Pleasure that your Lordship should transmit to the Plenipotentiaries at Lisle, by a Messenger whom I shall direct to be in readiness for that Purpose.

    (Signed) GRENVILLE.

Right Honourable
Lord Malmesbury.

(No. 51.)   Note from Lord Malmesbury to the French Plenipotentiaries.

Le Soussigné a rendu à sa Cour un Compte fidèle des Circonstances qui ont interrompu l'Exercice des Fonctions importantes qu'il avait plu au Roi son Maître de lui confier. Sa Majesté a daigné honorer de son Approbation entière les Réponses que le Soussigné a déjà faites à la Demande extraordinaire et inattendue que les nouveaux Plénipotentiaires de la République Française lui ont adressée dès leur Arrivée à Lille.

Mais pour ne laisser aucun Doute sur la Nature et l'Objet de cette Demande, le Soussigné a reçu l'Ordre exprès de déclarer au Nom de Sa Cour ;

1. Que les Plein-pouvoirs que Sa Majesté a jugé à propos de lui accorder pour traiter et conclure la Paix sont conçus et redigés dans la Forme la plus ample, autorisant le Soussigné pleinement et sans réserve à signer tout Traité de quelle Nature et sous quelles Conditions que ce fut, dont il pourrait convenir avec les Plénipotentiaires Français, en se conformant toujours aux Instructions qu'il aurait reçues de la part de Sa Cour.

2. Que ces Plein-pouvoirs ont été reçus et reconnus pour suffisans, tant par les Plénipotentiaires avec lesquels il a traité jusqu'ici, que par le Directoire lui-

lui-même ; et qu'il ne peut en conséquence y avoir Lieu à aucune nouvelle Discussion sur cet Objet déjà terminé par un commun Accord, et qui d'ailleurs n'est susceptible d'aucune Difficulté ou Doute quelconque ; tout ce qui a été fait à cet égard étant entièrement conforme aux Usages établis depuis long-tems, et reconnus par toutes les Nations de l'Europe.

3. Que la demande du Directoire se rapporte donc réellement, non pas aux Plein-pouvoirs du Soussigné mais à l'Etendue de ses Instructions, dont le Directoire ne pouvait, en aucun Cas, lui demander la Communication qu'en autant que le Soussigné pourrait la juger utile au Succès de la Négociation ; et que bien loin d'être dans le Cas de donner des nouvelles Explications quelconques, le Soussigné avait tout Lieu de croire, d'après les Communications réitérées qui lui ont été faites par les Plénipotentiaires Français, qu'il recevrait incessamment un Contre-Projet, de Nature à faciliter la Marche ultérieure de la Négociation suspendue depuis plus de Deux Mois.

4. Que la Cour de Londres a du être bien plus étonnée encore du Contenu de la nouvelle Demande faite au Soussigné ; cette Demande portant sur des Conditions Préliminaires qui avaient déjà été rejettées dès le Commencement de la Négociation, et dont les Plénipotentiaires Français s'étaient en Effet départis, per l'Annonce formelle des Mesures dont le Directoire s'occupait pour s'arranger en conséquence avec ses Alliés.

5. Que ce n'est donc qu'en consentant à traiter sur la Base du Projet détaillé avec tant de Franchise, que le Soussigné a remis dès les Premiers Jours de son Séjour à Lille, ou bien en lui faisant passer un Contre-Projet d'une Nature conciliatoire, conformément aux Assurances qu'il en a reçues depuis si long Tems, qu'il paraît possible de continuer la Négociation, dont les Plénipotentiares l'ont si fortement assuré que le Directoire ne désirait pas la Rupture,

malgré

malgré la Démarche adoptée à son égard, Démarche que le Soussigné s'abstient de qualifier, mais qui n'a pu manquer de produire ici l'Impression des Dispositions les moins pacifiques de la Part du Directoire.

Le Soussigné est chargé d'ajouter, que Sa Majesté verrait avec un vrai Regret la Certitude de ces Dispositions, si peu compatibles avec le Désir ardent qui l'anime, de pouvoir rendre la Paix aux Deux Nations ; mais que si sans y avoir contribué de Sa Part, Sa Majesté doit encore se trouver dans la Nécessité de continuer la Guerre, elle se conduira dans toutes les Occasions d'après les mêmes Principes, en faisant tout ce qui peut dépendre d'Elle pour le Rétablissement de la Paix, mais en persistant toujours à défendre, avec une Fermeté inébranlable, la Dignité de Sa Couronne et les Intérêts de Son Peuple.

Le Ministre Plénipotentiaire de Majesté Britannique prie les Ministres Plénipotentiaires de la République Française d'agréer l'Assurance de sa haute Considération.

(Signé) MALMESBURY.

A Londres,
ce 22 Septembre 1797.

(No. 51.) Translation.

THE Undersigned Minister Plenipotentiary of His Britannick Majesty has rendered to his Court a faithful Account of the Circumstances that have interrupted the Exercise of those important Functions which His Majesty has been pleased to entrust to him. His Majesty has deigned to honour with his entire Approbation the Answers which the Undersigned has already made to the extraordinary and unexpected Demands which the new Plenipotentiaries of the French Republick addressed to him immediately upon their Arrival at Lisle.

But in order to leave no Doubt respecting the Nature and Object of this Demand, the Undersigned has been expressly ordered to declare, in the Name of his Court:

1. That the full Powers with which His Majesty had thought proper to furnish him for negociating and concluding a Treaty of Peace, are conceived and expressed in the most ample Form, authorizing the Undersigned fully, and without Reserve, to sign any Treaty upon which he might agree with the French Plenipotentiaries whatever its Nature or Conditions might be; conforming himself in all Cases to the Instructions which he might receive from his Court.

2. That these full Powers have been received and recognized as sufficient, as well by the Plenipotentiaries with whom he has hitherto treated, as by the Directory themselves, and that there is consequently no Room for any new Discussion upon a Subject which has already been closed by common Agreement, and which moreover is not liable to any Doubt or Difficulty whatever; every Thing which has been done hitherto upon this Subject, being entirely conformable to Customs long established and recognized by all the Nations of Europe.

3. That the Demand of the Directory therefore, in Reality, refers not to the full Powers of the Undersigned, but to the Extent of his Instructions, of which the Directory could not, under any Circumstances, require any Communication, further than as the Undersigned himself might judge such a Communication conducive to the Success of the Negotiation; and that very far from being in a Situation to be called upon for any new Explanations whatever, the Undersigned had every Reason to expect, from the repeated Communications which had been made to him by the French Plenipotentiaries, that he should immediately receive a Contre-Projet, of a Nature to facilitate the further Progress of the Negotia-

gotiation which had been suspended for more than Two Months.

4. That the Court of London had good Reason to be still more astonished at the Substance of the new Demand made to the Undersigned; a Demand relating to Preliminary Conditions which had already been rejected at the very Commencement of the Negotiation, and from which the French Plenipotentiaries had in Effect departed, by a formal Notification of the Measures which the Directory were in consequence taking for the Purpose of coming to some Arrangement with their Allies.

5. That it is therefore only by consenting to treat upon the Basis of the Project, detailed with so much Openness, which was presented by the Undersigned a few Days after his Arrival at Lisle, or by returning a Contre-Projet of a conciliatory Nature, agreeably to the Assurances which he received so long ago, that it appears possible to continue the Negotiation, which the Plenipotentiaries have so strongly assured him that the Directory did not wish to break off, notwithstanding the Measures lately adopted with respect to him: A Measure which the Undersigned forbears to characterize, but which could not fail to produce in this Country the Impression of a Disposition by no Means pacifick on the Part of the Directory.

The Undersigned is directed to add, that His Majesty would see with real Regret the Certainty of the Existence of such a Disposition, so little compatible with the ardent Desire with which he is animated to restore Peace to the Two Nations; but that if, without having Himself contributed to it on His Part, He should again find Himself under the Necessity of continuing the War, He will conduct Himself upon every Occasion agreeably to the same Principles, doing every thing which can depend upon him for the Re-establishment of Peace, but

persisting

persisting to defend, with an unshaken Firmness, the Dignity of His Crown, and the Interests of His People.

The Minister Plenipotentiary of His Britannick Majesty requests the Ministers Plenipotentiary of the French Republick to accept the Assurance of his high Consideration.

    (Signed) MALMESBURY.

London,
[the 22d of September 1797.

(No. 52.) Note from the French Plenipotentiaries to Lord Malmesbury.

Les Ministres Plénipotentiaires de la République Française, chargés de traiter de la Paix avec l'Angleterre, ont reçu la Note, datée de Londres, qui leur a été apportée par un Courier extraordinaire, de la Part de Lord Malmesbury. Ils ont l'Honneur de lui répondre, que leur Note du 29 Fructidor, à laquelle ils se réfèrent, présentait la double Assurance de l'Intention formelle du Gouvernement Français de continuer les Négociations de la Paix, & de sa Détermination constante de n'accéder qu'à des Conventions compatibles avec la Dignité de la République Française.

Une Paix, dont la Base serait contraire aux Loix, ou aux Engagemens pris avec les Alliés, ne saurait remplir l'Espoir de la Nation. C'est un Point dont le Directoire Exécutif ne s'est jamais départi, & sur lequel ses Sentimens n'ont jamais varié.

Le Lord Malmesbury ayant formellement déclaré dans ses Notes des 15 & 24 Juillet, & en dernier Lieu du 17 Septembre, qu'il n'avait pas les Pouvoirs nécessaires pour restituer les Possessions Hollandaises & Espagnoles, occupées par les Troupes de Sa Majesté Britannique, le Directoire Exécutif a donné une nouvelle Preuve de sa loyale Franchise & de son Désir d'accélérer la Conclusion, en invitant le Lord

Lord Malmesbury à se retirer vers sa Cour, pour obtenir des Autorisations, sans lesquelles il ne peut pas conclure ; Démarche nécessité par les Déclarations du Ministre Plénipotentiaire de Sa Majesté Britannique, & sur laquelle il est impossible de faire prendre le Change à tout Esprit juste.

Les Ministres Plénipotentiaires de la République Française prient le Lord Malmesbury d'agréer les Assurances de leur haute Considération.

(Signé)   TREILHARD.
BONNIER.

Lille, le 4 Vendémiaire,
An 5 de la République.
(Sept. 25, 1797.)

Par les Ministres Plénipotentiaires,
le Sec. Gén. de la Légation,
DERCHÉ.

(No. 52.)   Translation.

The Ministers Plenipotentiary of the French Républick, commissioned to treat of Peace with England, have received the Note, dated from London, which has been brought to them by an extraordinary Messenger, from Lord Malmesbury. They have the Honour to answer to him, that their Note of the 29th Fructidor, to which they refer, offered the double Assurance of the settled Intention of the French Government to continue the Negotiations for Peace, and of its constant Determination not to agree to any other Conditions than such as are compatible with the Dignity of the French Republick.

A Peace, of which the Basis should be contrary to the Laws, or to the Engagements taken with its Allies, would never satisfy the Hopes of the Nation. It is a Point from which the Executive Directory has never departed, and upon which its Sentiments have never varied.

Lord Malmesbury having formally declared in his Notes of the 15th and 24th of July, and in the last Instance in that of the 17th September, that he had not the Powers necessary for restoring the Dutch and Spanish Possessions, occupied by the Troops of His Britannick Majesty, the Executive Directory has given a new Proof of its Openness, and of its Desire to accelerate the Conclusion of Peace, in requiring Lord Malmesbury to return to his Court, for the Purpose of obtaining the Authority, without which he cannot conclude; a Measure rendered necessary by the Declaration of the Minister Plenipotentiary of His Britannick Majesty, and upon which it is impossible to give a wrong Impression to any thinking and impartial Mind.

The Ministers Plenipotentiary of the French Republick request Lord Malmesbury to accept the Assurance of their high Consideration.

(Signed)   TREILHARD.
BONNIER.

Lisle, 4th Vendémiaire,
5th Year of the Republick,
(Sept. 25, 1797.)

DERCHÉ.

(No. 53.)   Note from the French Plenipotentiaries to Lord Malmesbury.

LES Ministres Plénipotentiaires de la République Française, chargés de traiter de la Paix avec l'Angleterre, ont l'Honneur de faire sçavoir au Lord Malmesbury, qu'aiant adressé Copie de sa dernière Note à son Gouvernement, le Directoire Exécutif leur a prescrit de déclarer en son Nom, qu'il n'a pas cessé de vouloir la Paix; qu'il a donné une Preuve non équivoque du Sentiment qui l'anime, lorsqu'il a ordonné aux Ministres Plénipotentiaires de la République de réclamer une Explication cathégorique sur les Pouvoirs donnés par le Gouvernement Anglais à son Ministre Plénipotentiaire; que cette Demande n'avait, et ne pouvait avoir, d'autre Objet, que d'amener enfin

enfin la Négociation à une Issue prompte et heureuse.

Que l'Ordre donné aux Ministres Plénipotentiaires de la République de rester à Lille après le Départ du Lord Malmesbury, est une nouvelle Preuve que le Directoire avait désiré et prévu son Retour. avec des Pouvoirs qui ne seraient pas Illusoires, et dont la Limitation ne serait plus un Prétexte pour retarder la Conclusion de la Paix.

Que telles sont toujours les Intentions et les Espérances du Directoire Exécutif, qui enjoint aux Ministres Plénipotentiaires de la République de ne quitter Lille, qu'au Moment où l'Absence prolongée du Négociateur ne laissera plus de Doute sur l'Intention de Sa Majesté Britannique de rompre toute Négociation.

Qu'en conséquence le vingt-cinq Vendémiaire courant (16 Octobre vieux style) est le Terme fixé pour le Rappel des Ministres Plénipotentiaires de la République Française, dans le Cas où à cette Epoque le Ministre Plénipotentiaire de Sa Majesté Britannique ne serait pas rendu à Lille.

Le Directoire Exécutif éprouvera un vif Regret qu'un Rapprochement déjà entamé deux fois n'ait pu être consommé ; mais sa Conscience et l'Europe entière lui rendront ce Témoignage, que le Gouvernement Anglais seul aura fait peser le Fléau de la Guerre sur les Deux Nations.

Les Ministres Plénipotentiaires de la République Française prient le Ministre Plénipotentiaire de Sa Majesté Britannique d'agréer les Assurances de leur haute Considération.

(Signé) TREILHARD.
BONNIER.

Lille, ce 10 Vendémiaire,
An 6, de la République Française.

Le Sécr. de la Légation,
Desché.

(No. 53.)   Translation.

THE Ministers Plenipotentiary of the French Republick, charged to treat for Peace with England, have the Honour to inform Lord Malmesbury, that having sent a Copy of his last Note to their Government, the Executive Directory has directed them to declare in its Name, That it has never ceased to wish for Peace; That it gave an unequivocal Proof of the Sentiment which animates it, when it ordered the Ministers Plenipotentiary of the Republick to require a categorical Explanation as to the Powers given by the English Government to its Minister Plenipotentiary; That this Demand had, and could have, no other Object but to bring the Negotiation to a speedy and successful Issue:

That the Order given to the Plenipotentiaries of the Republick to remain at Lisle after the Departure of Lord Malmesbury, is another Proof that the Directory had desired and foreseen his Return with Powers that should not be illusory, and the Limitation of which should no longer be a Pretext for delaying the Conclusion of Peace:

That such are still the Hopes and Intentions of the Executive Directory, which enjoins the Ministers Plenipotentiary of the Republick not to quit Lisle till the continued Absence of the Negotiator should no longer leave any Doubt of the Intention of His Britannick Majesty to break off all Negotiation:

That consequently the 25th Vendémiaire (16th of Octobre Old Style) is the Period fixed for the Recall of the Ministers Plenipotentiary of the French Republick, supposing that, at that Time, the Minister Plenipotentiary of His Britannick Majesty shall not have arrived at Lisle.

The Executive Directory will feel the greatest Regret that a Reconciliation, already twice attempted, should not be perfected; but its Conscience, and

3   the

the Whole of Europe, will bear it Testimony, that it is the English Government alone that will have inflicted the Scourge of War upon the Two Nations.

The Ministers Plenipotentiary of the French Republick entreat the Minister Plenipotentiary of His Britannick Majesty to accept the Assurances of their high Consideration.

     (Signed) TREILHARD.
            BONNIER.

Lisle, 10th Vendémiaire,
6th Year of the French Republick,
 (October 1, 1797.)

       The Sec. of the Legation,
           DERCHÉ.

(No. 54.) Note from Lord Malmesbury to the French Plenipotentiaries.

Le Soussigné ayant remis au Ministère du Roi la Note des Plénipotentiaires de la République Française, a l'ordre de leur observer,

Que ce n'est qu'en conséquence de l'Injonction formelle et positive du Directoire, qu'il a quitté Lille : que ses Pouvoirs n'étaient ni illusoires ni limités, et que rien n'a été omis de sa Part pour accélérer la Négociation, qui n'a été retardée que par les Délais du Directoire, et qui n'est aujourd'hui suspendue que par son Acte.

Pour ce qui regarde la Reprise des Conférences le Soussigné ne peut que se référer à sa dernière Note, où il a désigné avec Franchise et Précision les seuls Moyens qui restent pour continuer la Négociation : observant, en même Tems, que le Roi ne pourrait plus traiter en Pais Ennemi sans avoir la Certitude de voir respecter pour l'avenir dans la Personne de son Plénipotentiaire les Usages établis parmi toutes les Nations civilisées, à l'égard des Ministres Publics, et principalement de ceux chargés de travailler au Rétablissement de la Paix.

Le Ministre Plénipotentiaire de Sa Majesté Britannique prie les Ministres Plénipotentiaires de la République Française d'agréer les Assurances de sa haute Considération.

(Signé) MALMESBURY.

à Londres, ce 5 Octobre 1797.

(No. 54.) Translation.

THE Undersigned having laid before the King's Ministry the Note of the Plenipotentiaries of the French Republick, is directed to observe to them,

That it is only in consequence of the formal and positive Injunction of the Directory that he quitted Lisle; That his Powers were neither illusory nor limited; And that nothing was omitted on his Part to accelerate the Negotiation, which has been only retarded by the Delays of the Directory, and which at this Moment is only suspended by its Act.

With regard to the Renewal of the Conferences, the Undersigned can only refer to his last Note, where he has explained with Frankness and Precision the only Means which remain for continuing the Negotiation; observing, at the same Time, that the King could no longer treat in an Enemy's Country, without being certain that the Customs established amongst all civilized Nations, with regard to Publick Ministers, and especially to those charged to negotiate for the Re-establishment of Peace, would be respected for the future in the Person of His Plenipotentiary.

The Minister Plenipotentiary of His Britannick Majesty requests the Ministers Plenipotentiary of the French Republick to accept the Assurance of his high Consideration.

(Signed) MALMESBURY.

London, 5th October, 1797.

Feb.y 1804.

I have been assured by one lately in a very confidential situation that all this negotiat.n betw. L.d Melm.th & the Plenip.s of the Directory at Lisle was a farce, to masque the real negotiat.n wh.

DECLARATION

was secretly carrying on at the same time by a private Agent of Minis: :ters — that the principal points of this the real negotiation were nearly arranged, when the

OF THE COURT OF GREAT BRITAIN,

Triumvirate upon obtaining complete success in the Revolution of September altered their whole

RESPECTING THE LATE

determination in regard to Peace with England, & resolved upon the rupture which soon after

NEGOTIATION.

followed — This person added sign.t "George Ellis" (He was L.d M.g.s Secr.y at L.) "can tell you a good deal upon that subject. —

LONDON:
PRINTED FOR J. WRIGHT, NO. 169, PICCADILLY,
OPPOSITE OLD BOND-STREET.

1797.

DECLARATION.

[PUBLISHED BY HIS MAJESTY'S COMMAND.]

His Majesty's benevolent endeavours to restore to his People the Blessings of secure and honourable Peace, again repeated without success, have again demonstrated beyond the possibility of doubt, the determined and persevering hostility of the Government of France, <u>in whose unprovoked aggression the War originated</u>, and by whose boundless and destructive Ambition it is still prolonged. And while by the course of these transactions, continued proofs have been afforded to all his Majesty's faithful Subjects, of his anxious and unremitting solicitude for their welfare, they cannot, at the same time, have failed to recognize, in the uniform conduct of the Enemy, the spirit by which the Councils of France are still actuated, and the objects to which they are directed.

His Majesty could not but feel how much the means of Peace had been obstructed by the many additional difficulties which his Enemies had so repeatedly thrown in the way of every Negotiation. Nevertheless, on the very first appearance of circumstances in some degree more favourable to the interests of humanity, the same ardent desire for the ease and happiness of his Subjects, induced his Majesty to renew his overtures for terminating the calamities of War: thus availing himself of every opening which could in any manner lead to secure and honourable Peace, and consulting equally the wishes of his own heart, and the principles by which his conduct has invariably been guided.

New obstacles were immediately interposed by those who still directed the Councils of France, and who, amidst the general desire for Peace, which they could not at that time openly disclaim, still retained the power of frustrating the wishes of their own country, of counteracting his Majesty's benevolent intentions, and of obstructing that result, which was so necessary for the happiness of both nations. Difficulties of form were studiously created; modes of Negotiation were insisted upon, the most inconsistent with their own conduct in every other instance; the same spirit appeared in every step which was taken by them; and while the most unwarranted

× This alludes to the Message of Directory aftr wh: Ld. M. reclaimed. See p.

[5]

<u>insinuations were thrown out</u>, and <u>the most unfounded reproaches</u>×brought forward, the established customs and usages, which have long prevailed in Europe, were purposely departed from, even in the simplest acts which were to be done on their part for the renewal of the Negotiations. All these things his Majesty determined to disregard; not as being insensible of their purport and tendency, nor unmindful of the importance of these points, in the public intercourse of great and independent nations, but resolving to defeat the object of these artifices, and to suffer no subordinate or inferior consideration to impede, on his part, the discussion of the weighty and extensive interests on which the termination of the War must necessarily depend.

He directed his Minister to repair to France, furnished with the most ample powers, and instructed to communicate at once an explicit and detailed proposal and plan of Peace, reduced into the shape of a regular Treaty, just and moderate in its principles, embracing all the interests concerned, and extending to every subject connected with the restoration of public tranquillity. The communication of this Paper, delivered in the very first conference, was accompanied by such explanations as fully stated and detailed the utmost extent of his Majesty's views, and at the same time gave ample room for the examination of every disputed point, for mutual arrangement and concession, and for reciprocal facilities arising out of the progress of fair discussion.

'To this proceeding, open and liberal beyond example, the conduct of his Majesty's Enemies opposes the most striking contrast. From them no Counter-project has ever yet been obtained: no statement of the extent or nature of the conditions on which they would conclude any Peace with these Kingdoms. Their pretensions have always been brought forward either as detached or as preliminary points, distinct from the main object of Negotiation, and accompanied, in every instance, with an express reserve of farther and unexplained demands.

The points which, in pursuance of this system, the Plenipotentiaries of the Enemy proposed for separate discussion in their first conferences with his Majesty's Minister, were at once frivolous and offensive*; none of them productive of any solid advantage to France, but all calculated to raise new obstacles in the way of Peace. And to these demands was soon after added another, in its form unprecedented, in its substance extravagant, and such as could originate only in the most determined and inveterate hostility. The principle of mutual compensation, before expressly admitted by common consent, as the

[handwritten annotation]

[7]

just and equitable basis of Negotiation, was now disclaimed; every idea of moderation or reason, every appearance of justice, was disregarded; and a concession was required from his Majesty's Plenipotentiary, as a preliminary and indispensable condition of Negotiation, which must at once have superseded all the objects, and precluded all the means of treating. France, after incorporating with her own dominions so a large a portion of her conquests, and affecting to have deprived herself, by her own internal regulations, of the power of alienating these valuable additions of territory, did not scruple to demand from his Majesty the absolute and unconditional surrender of all that the energy of his People, and the Valour of his Fleets and Armies, have conquered in the present War, either from France or from her Allies. She required that the power of Great Britain should be confined within its former limits, at the very moment when her own dominion was extended to a degree almost unparalleled in history. She insisted, that in proportion to the increase of danger, the means of resistance should be diminished; and that his Majesty should give up, without compensation, and into the hands of his Enemies, the necessary defences of his possessions, and the future safeguards of his empire. Nor was even this demand brought forward as constituting the terms of Peace, but the price of Negotiation;

※ *Non constat — S:r M. was required only to declare y:t he was invested with full Powers to make su[ch] Restitution of it as sh:d demanded — He was not req:d in the 1:st instance [8] to make such restitut:n*

as the condition on which alone his Majesty was to be allowed to learn what further unexplained demands were still reserved, and to what greater sacrifices these unprecedented concessions of honour and safety were to lead. ✗ *How so!*

"Whatever were the impressions which such a proceeding created, they did not induce the King abruptly to preclude the means of Negotiation. In rejecting without a moment's hesitation a demand, which could have been made for no other reason than because it was inadmissible, his Majesty, from the fixed resolution to avail himself of every chance of bringing the Negotiation to a favourable issue, directed that an opening should still be left for treating on reasonable and equal grounds, such as might become the dignity of his Crown, and the rank and station in Europe in which it has pleased the Divine Providence to place the British Nation. *but from which it has pleased our divine Minister to degrade it.*

"This temperate and conciliatory conduct was strongly expressive of the benevolence of his Majesty's intentions; and it appeared for some time to have prepared the way for that result which has been the uniform object of all his measures. Two months elapsed after his Majesty had unequivocally and definitively refused to comply with the unreasonable and extravagant Preliminary which had been de-

✗ *Observe this confess:n y:t it was inadmis:sibly, even from the first, & at all events. And yet Ministers have said in Parliam:t that if the Directory had conducted y:mselves reasonably they (Min:rs) w:d have ceded every thing for Peace —*

manded by his Enemies. During all that time the Negotiation was continued open, the conferences were regularly held, and the demand thus explicitly rejected by one party, was never once renewed by the other. It was not only abandoned; it was openly disclaimed; assurances were given in direct contradiction to it. Promises were continually repeated, that his Majesty's explicit and detailed proposals should at length be answered by that which could alone evince a real disposition to negotiate with sincerity, by the delivery of a Counter-project, of a nature tending to facilitate the conclusion of Peace; and the long delays of the French Government in executing these promises were excused and accounted for by an unequivocal declaration, that France was concerting with her Allies for those sacrifices on their part, which might afford the means of proceeding in the Negotiation. Week after week passed over in the repetition of these solemn engagements on the part of his Majesty's Enemies. His desire for Peace induced him to wait for their completion, with an anxiety proportioned to the importance of the object; nor was it much to expect that his Minister should at length be informed what was the extent and nature of the conditions on which his Enemies were disposed to terminate the War.

It was in this stage of the business that, on

the 11th of September, the appointment of new Plenipotentiaries was announced on the part of France, under a formal promise that their arrival should facilitate and expedite the work of Peace.

To renew, in a shape still more offensive than before, the <u>inadmissible</u> demand so long before brought forward, and so long abandoned, was the first act of these new Messengers of Peace. And such was now the undisguised impatience of the King's Enemies to terminate all treaty, and to exclude all prospect of accommodation, that even the continuance of the King's Plenipotentiary at the appointed place of Negotiation was made by them to depend on his immediate compliance with a condition which his Court had, two months before, explicitly refused, and concerning which no farther discussion had since occurred. His reply was such as the occasion required: and he immediately received a positive and written order to depart from France.

The subsequent conduct of his Majesty's Enemies has aggravated even this proceeding, and added fresh insult to this unexampled outrage. The insurmountable obstacles which they threw in the way of Peace were accompanied with an ostentatious profession of the most pacific dispositions. In cutting off the means of Negotiation, they still pretended to retain the strongest desire to negotiate: in ordering the King's Minister to quit their country, they professed the hope of his immediate return to it. And in renewing their former inadmissible and rejected demand, they declared their confident expectation of a speedy and favourable answer. Yet before any answer could arrive, they published a Declaration, announcing to their country the departure of the King's Minister; and attempting, as in every former instance, to ascribe to the conduct of Great Britain the disappointment of the general wish for Peace, and the renewal of all the calamities of War. The same attempt has been prolonged in subsequent Communications, equally insidious and illusory, by which they have obviously intended to furnish the colour and empty pretence of a wish for Peace, while they have still studiously and obstinately persisted in evading every step which could lead to the success of any Negotiation; have continued to insist on the same inadmissible and extravagant Preliminary, and have uniformly withheld all explanation, either on the particulars of the Proposals of Peace, so long since delivered by his Majesty's Minister, or on any other terms on which they were themselves ready to conclude: and this in the vain hope, that it could be possible by any artifice to disguise the truth of these transactions, or that any exercise of power, however despotic, could prevent such facts from being known, felt, and understood, even in France itself.

To France, to Europe, and to the world, it must be manifest, that the French Government (while they persist in their present sentiments) leave his Majesty without any alternative, unless he were prepared to surrender and sacrifice to the undisguised Ambition of his Enemies, the Honour of his Crown and the Safety of his Dominions. It must be manifest that, instead of shewing on their part, any inclination to meet his Majesty's pacific overtures on any moderate terms, they have never brought themselves to state any terms (however exorbitant) on which they were ready to conclude Peace. They have asked as a Preliminary (and in the form the most arrogant and offensive) Concessions, which the comparative situation of the two Countries would have rendered extravagant in any stage of Negotiation; which were directly contrary to their own repeated professions; and which nevertheless, they peremptorily required to be complied with in the very outset; reserving an unlimited power of afterwards accumulating, from time to time, fresh demands, increasing in proportion to every new Concession.

On the other hand, the Terms proposed by his Majesty have been stated in the most clear, open, and unequivocal manner. The discussion of all the points to which they relate, or of any others, which the Enemy might bring forward as the Terms of Peace, has been, on his Majesty's part, repeatedly called for, as often promised by the French Plenipotentiaries, but to this day has never yet been obtained. The rupture of the Negotiation is not, therefore, to be ascribed to any pretensions (however inadmissible) urged *as the Price of Peace;* not to any ultimate difference *on Terms,* however exorbitant; but to the evident and fixed determination of the Enemy to prolong the contest, and to pursue, at all hazards, their hostile designs against the prosperity and safety of these Kingdoms.

While this determination continues to prevail, his Majesty's earnest wishes and endeavours to restore Peace to his Subjects must be fruitless. But his sentiments remain unaltered. He looks with anxious expectation to the moment when the Government of France may shew a disposition and spirit in any degree corresponding to his own. And he renews, even now, and before all Europe, the solemn Declaration, that, in spite of repeated provocations, and at the very moment when his claims have been strengthened and confirmed by that fresh success which, by the Blessing of Providence, has recently attended his arms, he is yet ready (if the calamities of War can now be closed) to conclude Peace on the same mo-

ine gives us a curious account of the
agant pretensions & demands of the Hol.
rs, when Louis 14th, in his turn, was
ated at their feet, suing for peace — And
es most truly, for his countrymen have-

derate and equitable principles and terms which he has before proposed: the rejection of such terms must now, more than ever, demonstrate the implacable animosity, and insatiable ambition* of those with whom he has to contend, and to them alone must the future consequences of the prolongation of the War be ascribed.

If such, unhappily, is the spirit by which they are still actuated, his Majesty can neither hesitate as to the principles of his own conduct, nor doubt the sentiments and determination of his People. He will not be wanting to them, and he is confident they will not be wanting to themselves. He has an anxious, but a sacred and indispensable duty to fulfil: he will discharge it with resolution, constancy, and firmness. Deeply as he must regret the continuance of a War, so destructive in its progress, and so burthensome even in its success, he knows the character of the brave People whose Interests and Honour are entrusted to him. These it is the first object of his life to maintain: and he is convinced; that neither the Resources nor the Spirit of his Kingdoms will be found inadequate to this arduous contest, or unequal to the importance and value of the objects which are at stake. He trusts that the Favour of Providence, by which they have always hitherto been supported against all their Enemies, will be still extended to

proved the truth of the observation, that "L'esprit républicain est au fond aussi ambitieux que l'esprit monarchique."

[15]

them; and that, under this protection, his faithful Subjects, by a resolute and vigorous application of the means which they possess, will be enabled to vindicate the Independence of their Country, and to resist with just indignation the <u>assumed superiority</u> of an Enemy, *impudent* against whom they have fought with the courage, and success, and glory of their Ancestors, and who aims at nothing less than to destroy at once whatever has contributed to the prosperity and greatness of the British Empire: all the channels of its industry, and all the sources of its power; its security from abroad, its tranquillity at home; and, above all, that <u>Constitution</u>, on which alone depends the undisturbed enjoyment of its Religion, Laws, and Liberties. —

note this up: or to

Mr Mongis declares: "That the French Rep.c & the English Gov.t c.d not exist together." this was on the 31.st of October: see my note b: 97. d.p.80.

Westminster, Oct. 25, 1797.

This Day is published, Price Three Shillings,

FRENCH AGGRESSION;

PROVED FROM

MR. ERSKINE'S "VIEW OF THE CAUSES OF THE
"WAR;"

WITH REFLECTIONS

ON THE ORIGINAL CHARACTER OF THE FRENCH REVOLUTION, AND ON THE SUPPOSED DURABILITY
OF THE FRENCH REPUBLIC.

BY JOHN BOWLES, ESQ.

"Oh that mine Adversary had written a Book."
JOB.

SECOND EDITION, WITH ADDITIONS.

" This Pamphlet contains, not only a refutation of a
" peculiar kind, of the principal points contended for in
" Mr. Erskine's publication; a refutation, drawn from the
" most satisfactory of all sources, the admissions of the Au-
" thor himself; but offers also many pertinent and impor-
" tant observations, respecting the present awful period,
" highly interesting to every man who has any thing at
" stake, in the great contest now depending."

BRITISH CRITIC, October, 1797.

www.ingramcontent.com/pod-product-compliance
Lightning Source LLC
Chambersburg PA
CBHW022129160426
43197CB00009B/1210